A Killer Unleashed

The "Spanish Flu" Pandemic on the Eastern Shore of Virginia

Other books you might enjoy

Books by Robert and Patricia Smiley

	**Frankford Heroes** A tribute to the 142 soldiers from the Frankford neighborhood of Philadelphia who gave their lives in service to their country from the Civil War to the current day.
	**Frankford Stories** A collection of stories published in the Frankford Gazette. The common thread is that the stories are told by our readers.
	**Frankford People** A neighborhood is not land or buildings, it is the people. This is a collection of stories about the people of Frankford, That were published in the Frankford Gazette from 2009 through 2019.

For more information, go to: www.smileypublishing.org

For the best Computer Programming Books, visit our friends at
John Smiley Publishing
http://www.johnsmiley.com/main/mybooks.htm

A Killer Without Mercy

The "Spanish Flu" Pandemic on the Eastern Shore of Virginia

Robert F. Smiley
Patricia M. Smiley

Smiley Publishing
2021

Copyright © 2021 by Robert F. Smiley and Patricia M. Smiley

All rights reserved. This book or any portion thereof may not be reproduced or used in any manner whatsoever without the express written permission of the publisher except for the use of brief quotations in a book review or scholarly journal.

First Printing: 2021

ISBN 9798456876287

Smiley Publishing
Post Office Box 453
Chincoteague, VA 23336-0453

www.smileypublishing.org
smile138@gmail.com

    Photo on the cover and page 17 is the Emergency hospital during the influenza epidemic at Camp Funston, Kansas (1918). Original image from National Museum of Health and Medicine. Digitally enhanced by rawpixel.com.

Dedication

This book is dedicated to the Doctors and caregivers of Virginia's Eastern Shore. The doctors made house calls to rich and poor alike, often exposing themselves and their families to the worst sickness anyone had ever seen. They are known to us from the official records and their names are listed below.

However, it was the caregivers who bore the greatest burden of nursing and caring for these very sick people. For the most part, their names will never be known.

Doctor Nathaniel Smith of Chincoteague out on house calls sometime in the early 1900s. Photo credit to "Chincoteague Island: A History of Local Business" / James Waine Carpenter, Sr.

Edward Alacott, MD - Onancock
John Hack Ayres, MD - Accomac
Emory Everett Bell, MD - Chincoteague
John William Bowdoin, MD - Bloxom
William Meade Burwell, MD - Chincoteague
William Lee Cosby, MD - Painter
William Lee Dalby, MD - Bridgetown
Joseph L. DeCormis, MD - Accomac
John D. Dickerson, MD - Stockton, Maryland
Edmund W. P. Downing, MD - Franktown
Fletcher Drummond, MD - Parksley

S. U. Fields, MD - Cape Charles
Oscar Richard (Frank) Fletcher, MD - Sanford
George Lee Fosque, MD - Onancock
R. W. Garrett, MD - Richmond
George Gill, MD - Camp Lee
Bertram Hensel Gilmer, MD - Cape Charles
Charles Frederick Gladstone, MD - Tangier
Charles M. Graden, MD - Temperanceville
Griffin W. Holland, MD - Eastville
John T. B. Hyslup, MD - Belle Haven
J. Walker Jackson, MD - Machipongo
J. W. Kellam, MD - Onley
Sydney Sheppard Kellam, MD - Belle Haven
William Finney Kellam, MD - Onley
William W. Kerns, MD - Bloxom
James W. Lankford, MD - New Church
J. H. A. Lofland, MD - Melfa
C. L. Lum, MD - Cape Charles
J. M. Lynch, MD - Cape Charles
Edward Thomas Mason, MD - Savageville
Alva Adair Matthews, MD - Oak Hall
Burleigh Nichols Mears, MD - Belle Haven
Daniel Webster Palmer, MD - Cape Charles
R. D. Parks, MD - Parksley
Oscar Littleton Powell, MD - Onancock
Charles Martin Reid, MD - Exmore
Edgar Waples Robertson, MD - Onancock
Nathaniel S. Smith, MD - Chincoteague
William J. Sturgis, MD - Franktown
Garland M. Vaden, MD - Townsend
L. M. Walker, MD - Eastville
A. E. West, MD - Nandua
Robert W. White, MD - Chincoteague
Rooker White, MD - Keller
J. Y. York, MD - Cheriton

Contents

Dedication 5
Notes 10
Acknowledgements 11
Preface 12
Introduction 13
1918 "Spanish Flu" Pandemic 14
Chapter 1 – It Begins 18
Chapter 2 – It Explodes 20
Chapter 3 – It Burns 37
Chapter 4 – Holiday Grief 45
Chapter 5 – Beginning of the End 56
Chapter 6 – The Cool Down 63
Chapter 7 – The End 66
Appendix I - Methodology 69
Appendix II – Demographics 74
Appendix III – Alphabetical Index 75
Appendix IV - Cemetery Index 82
Appendix V – Death Notices 90
   Louise Turlington Mapp 90
   Cecil George Washington Monds 90
   Frisby Ray Bowden 91
   Severin Paul Babin 91
   Orlin Q. Davis 92
   Ellison Ricketts Doughty 92
   William E. Andrews 92
   John Wilson Mumford 93
   Robert Franklin Bull 94
   Harry Absolom Phipps 95
   Melnyda A. Milligan 95
   James Herbert Ward 95

Margaret E. Whealton Bishop	96
Colie Sydney Hutchinson	96
Mildred W. Oldrich	96
Ella D. (Elodie) Lynch Russell	96
Susan Galena Russell	97
Annie Elizabeth Tolbert	97
Garland Beach Downing	97
Willie Wright Wessells	98
Alonzo Eugene Matthews	98
Addie Virginia Lewis	99
Gay Patterson Somers	99
Jesse Bonnewell	100
William Tankard Belote	100
Clarence Elton Burch	100
Charles Anderton Grace Westcott	101
Pearl Mears Bundick	101
Joshua David Malone	101
Lafayette Robins	102
Eva May White	102
Susan Rebecca Robins	102
Anna Laura Nordstrom	103
Clifford Arrington Nottingham	103
Leonard Joseph Stevens	103
Washington Hunt	104
Georgie T. Phillips	104
Eunice Parks	105
Herbert Burton Parsons	105
Edith Mae Beatty	106
Lula V. Jester	106
Claud J. Matthews	107
Mary C. Andrews	107
Joseph Kellam	108
Annie Eliza Davis	108
Mary Ann Martin	109
Olevia May Steelman	110
Charlotte Alice Gladding	111
Margaret and Ione Scott	111
Fannie Thomas Bell	112
Thomas C. Carpenter	112

Ansley Hopkins 112
References 113
Epilogue 114

Notes

All place names are in Virginia unless otherwise indicated. Some towns no longer exist as such.

Medical terms are transcribed from the death certificates.

*Indicates the individual was identified as Black, Colored or Mulatto on their death certificate.

Acknowledgements

This research would not have been possible without the help of many people. Thanks to:

Stacia Childers - Eastern Shore Public Library
Maria Grenchik Cathell - Museum of Chincoteague
Ellen Johnson and John Bates - Eastern Shore Railway Museum
Cindy Faith – Step Through Time Tours of Chincoteague
Sandra Schisler - Christ United Methodist Church
James Waine Carpenter, Sr.
Joseph W. Smiley, M.D.
John D. Smiley
Theodore Snotherly
Edward Zantek
Ron Sauder – Secant Publishing
Roberta Hyman - Photo of Robert Sacks
Charles Kelly - Photo of Harry Phipps
Kimberly Leffler - Photo of Carrie Manning
Clara Thomas - Photo of John William Kelley

Preface

In the midst of the COVID-19 pandemic, while riding it out at home here in Chincoteague in 2020, my curiosity was piqued about how this area fared during the Spanish Flu (H1N1 Influenza A virus) epidemic of 1918. There are some clear parallels with the present time.

As I waded deeper into this story, I wrote a profile of each person and included everything that would help to know who that person was. It soon became apparent to me as I accumulated data that poverty was a significant factor in who survived the Flu.

Race was something that I would have preferred to ignore thinking that it was not relevant but that was naive. Poverty did play a part in whether a person lived or died from the Flu and Race was very much linked to poverty. I have coded each individual who was identified on their death certificate as Black, Colored or Mulatto with an asterisk after their name. The reader can then read the stories and come to their own conclusion.

The deaths are listed in chronological order to show how the flu developed. Appendix III is an alphabetical index for those searching for a particular name. Appendix IV are images of the death notices which were a significant source of material.

Introduction

In 1918, the world had been at war for almost four years, but it was not until April of 1917, that the United States entered the war. Mobilization took time and the training of troops began. In March of 1918, in an Army training camp, reports of the Flu began to emerge. It spread throughout the Army camps rapidly. As the soldiers were shipped, they carried the virus with them and soon it engulfed Europe. The first phase of the Flu diminished in the Summer.

Troops began returning in the Fall and the first report of the Flu in this area was from Camp Lee near Petersburg in September. This more deadly version of the Flu moved into the civilian population easily and spread to the Eastern Shore by the end of September.

The Flu had eventually killed 675,000 Americans when it finally died out in the Spring of 1919. Over 200 of those people lived here, on the Eastern Shore of Virginia in Accomack and Northampton Counties. What follows is the story of those who perished.

1918 "Spanish Flu" Pandemic

I am not a historian and to write a comprehensive history of this event is beyond my capabilities. I am a researcher and when I find something interesting, I try to find the facts. What follows is my take on the facts of what I found to be important about the events and the people involved.

This pandemic was called the "Spanish Flu" at the time but the historic record links it to the Influenza outbreak that first appeared in the Army camps in Kansas in the Spring of 1918. Those soldiers were in training for deployment to France for combat in World War I.

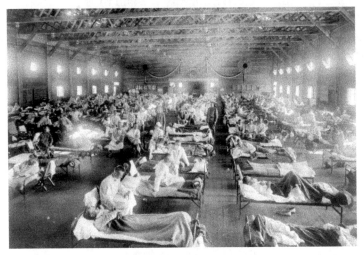

Camp Funston, at Fort Riley, Kansas, during the 1918 Spanish flu pandemic

They may have carried the virus with them to France, where it went on to infect massive numbers of troops and likely developed into a more lethal strain which they then carried back with returning troops to the U.S.A.

It was given the moniker "Spanish Flu" because although it turned up all over Europe, every country except Spain was under wartime censorship. The only place where it was reported in the news was in Spain and hence the name applied. Knowing what we know now, it might have just as well have been called the Kansas Flu.

There was a constant stream of troops going to France and returning home. In September, at Camp Lee, this Flu returned in a new, deadlier mutation and began to spread.

The first deaths recorded on the Eastern shore were in September when two students, who had been at school on the mainland, and one resident of Northampton County, died.

In October, it exploded and was all over, up and down the peninsula. It was everywhere all at once and then gradually diminished until March of 1919 when the last deaths were seen. Based on death certificates, I can account for 211 people who died of Influenza.

The victims did not directly die of Influenza, they died of things brought on by Influenza, most often Bacterial Pneumonia.

There was little in the way of treatment and vaccines were a few years away. For most people, the doctor came and did what he could. The disease held them in its grip for sometimes as long as two weeks before finally killing them. There was a shortage of both doctors and nurses due to the War in Europe and there was not yet a hospital on Virginia's Eastern Shore.

The median age at death for white residents was 27 years old. The median age at death for Black residents was 15. A more detailed analysis might indicate that poverty was the most significant factor in the difference. You will see from reading the individual cases that the Black residents were more likely to have died without seeing a doctor and there are a significant number of multiple fatalities within the same family.

The Spanish Flu in the United States killed at a very high rate. If the Corona virus killed at the same rate as the Spanish Flu, today we would have over 2,000,000 dead.

Are there any lessons to be learned from how the Spanish Flu epidemic was fought?

- The debates about masks are quite similar between the two periods. The lesson is that it's hard to tell Americans what to do. Some will follow the advice and others will not.
- Leadership during the Spanish Flu epidemic came almost entirely at the local level. President Wilson felt constrained about making any comment about the issue due to National Security concerns since it was wartime and to admit that there was a crisis at home would be an

admission of weakness. During the Corona virus crisis the messaging from the National Government was often mixed. In addition, the scientists initially did a poor job of explaining the science.
- Restriction on travel and the closure of public spaces was recognized during both periods as an important tool for stopping the spread. People supported and opposed it at similar rates, but the decisions rested primarily with local authorities during the Spanish Flu.
- Mask mandates were also a point of contention during both periods.

When I first started looking at the spread of the "Spanish Flu", I was surprised at how fast it traveled. My thinking was that travel was more difficult during that time. There were no highways and local travel was in many cases by horse and buggy.

What I did not realize was the importance of the railroads on the Eastern Shore and the ease of travel that they offered. It was possible to get on the train in Cape Charles in the morning and be in Philadelphia in time for dinner. That train also stopped at every town and village of any size along the way. Philadelphia was one of the most infected cities in the country and it became clear that the spread must have been made easier by the railroad. There was no place safe from the Flu.

Chapter 1 – It Begins

September 1918

Doctor William Finney Kellam was 38 that morning in late September as he scanned the Peninsula Enterprise, the local weekly newspaper. There was no hint of the pandemic on the horizon, only news of the war still raging in France.

He was a resident of Onley and he would treat many patients with Influenza in the months to come. He holds the unfortunate record of having seen the most deaths among the 46 doctors who signed death certificates during the epidemic. He was a 1902 graduate of Randolph-Macon College and a 1906 graduate of Johns Hopkins University for his medical degree. He was as prepared as any doctor could have been to fight a disease that had no cure.

People on the Eastern Shore had heard about the Flu that was infecting the soldiers over at Camp Lee, but it was not the big news of the day. War news dominated the newspapers on the Eastern Shore. President Wilson's administration made a point to downplay the Flu because of concerns that it would give the appearance that the United States might not be up to the task of waging the war in Europe.

Residents had sons and daughters over on the mainland in schools and also in the Army camps. Families would often go over to visit. It was an easy trip from Cape Charles over to Norfolk. People and freight moved freely and often, up and down the Eastern Shore during this period. It was also an easy trip on the train up to Philadelphia for shopping. This constant flow of people made the Eastern Shore vulnerable to the spread of the virus.

In September, there were 3 deaths, two of those were students over on the mainland. Thomas Harman was the first Eastern Shore resident to die on the peninsula.

Louise Turlington Mapp - The first death to touch Accomack County was 17-year-old Louise who had left home to begin studies at Hollins College in Salem in early in September. Not long after she left for school, her parents were notified that she was sick, and they immediately left to visit her. She was receiving medical care from September 23rd until she died on **September 26th** of Bronchial Pneumonia following Influenza.

She was survived by her father, William, a truck farmer, her mother Mary, and a younger sister, Emma. Louise was mourned by the entire community at her funeral at the Garrisons Methodist Church in Painter.

The family lived in Mappsburg, and she was buried in Belle Haven Cemetery.

Thomas Harman* - Thomas was a 43-year-old sawmill laborer. He was a tall man with a medium build and he was the first fatality in Northampton County when he died on **September 28th** at Jamesville, of Influenza following Pneumonia. He had not been seen by Doctor C. M. Reid, but he determined the cause of death based on information from his family. Thomas was survived by his mother Marianne Ames. His father George had predeceased him. Thomas was buried in Occohannock Cemetery in Belle Haven.

George Washington Cecil Monds - George was a 17-year-old student at the Forks Union Military Academy in Forks Union, when he was stricken with the flu. He was under the care of a doctor from September 27th until **September 29th** when he died of pneumonia following Influenza.

The family home was in **Mappsville,** at the time of his death. He was survived by his father, Riley S. Monds, stepmother, Margaret, brothers, Riley and Alvah, and a sister, Maude. His mother, Maude had predeceased him in 1915. He was buried in Bethel Baptist Church Cemetery.

Chapter 2 – It Explodes

October 1918

Doctor Oscar Richard Fletcher was 36 years old when the epidemic began. He was practicing medicine from his home in Sanford, on the Sanford/Saxis Road. He was born in Jenkins Bridge and graduated from the University of Maryland School of Medicine in 1908.

Doctor Fletcher called on the home of Robert Bull on October 1st. When he died on October 11th, he was the first of eight of his patients who would die of the disease.

The Flu exploded on the Eastern Shore in October with 77 deaths in total as officials began to take action to prevent the spread of the virus. It appeared everywhere almost immediately.

On October 2nd, the Board of Health of Accomack County ordered the closure of "Moving Picture Shows" and requested that churches cease protracted meetings at night.

In the Peninsula Enterprise, the weekly newspaper, they published a notice that ordered all stores and barber shops to close by 7 PM in the evening. Churches were requested to not hold services until conditions improved. In regard to schools, they noted that when the number of absent sick children was great, schools had already closed, so the decision was left to the local authority.

In addition, they offered some guidance on avoiding the Flu, but it spread like wildfire. It took rich and poor alike. There was no hospital on the Eastern Shore at this time. Treatment options were extremely limited. The victims died of bacterial pneumonia in almost all cases which was brought on by the flu.

In the present day, the patient might be prescribed an antibiotic to help with the pneumonia, but antibiotics did not appear for another 10 years.

Aspirin was in common use but was often prescribed in what are now considered to be toxic doses. Some victims of the Flu may have in fact died from aspirin toxicity.

TREASURY DEPARTMENT
UNITED STATES PUBLIC HEALTH SERVICE

INFLUENZA

Spread by Droplets sprayed from Nose and Throat

Cover each COUGH and SNEEZE with handkerchief.

Spread by contact.

AVOID CROWDS.

If possible, WALK TO WORK.

Do not spit on floor or sidewalk.

Do not use common drinking cups and common towels.

Avoid excessive fatigue.

If taken ill, go to bed and send for a doctor.

The above applies also to colds, bronchitis, pneumonia, and tuberculosis.

Frisby Rayfield Bowden - Ray Bowden, a 25-year-old Oysterman from **Chincoteague**, died at Camp Lee of Influenza on **October 2nd**. He had been inducted into the Army in May for training to be shipped out to France.

He was survived by his father, John P. Bowden and three brothers who lived at 289 Main Street. He was buried in Greenwood Cemetery in Chincoteague.

Nettie Thelma Johnson - Nettie was 27 years old and married to Ellison Castin Johnson, living in **Wardtown**. She was suffering with Tuberculosis but caught the Flu and was under the care of Doctor Kellam from September 28th until **October 2nd** when she died.

She was survived by her husband, son, John, her parents, John and Georgianna Killman, and a brother, Otho. She was buried in Franktown Cemetery.

Orlin Q. Davis - Popular young Orlin, 18 years old of **Chincoteague**, died of Influenza in Wilmington, Delaware where he was working at the Harlan Plant of Bethlehem Ship Building in Delaware on **October 3rd**.

He was survived by his father, Quinton an oysterman, mother Annie, and three sisters who lived at 223 Church Street in Chincoteague. He was buried in Whatcoat United Methodist Church Cemetery in Snow Hill, Maryland.

Ellison Rickets Doughty - Ellison (Ricks) was a 34-year-old, married, father of 3, a dock carpenter, working for Partrus Brothers. They lived in **Willis Wharf** when he came down with the Flu. He was under the care of Doctor Downing from September 26th until **October 4th** when he died of Pneumonia following Influenza. He was buried in the Epworth Methodist Church Cemetery (also known as Broadwater Church Cemetery) in Exmore.

William E. Andrews - William was a 15-year-old schoolboy when he was stricken by influenza on September 27th. He struggled on until **October 7th** when he died. Doctor White said a weak heart contributed to his death. The family lived "Down the Marsh" in **Chincoteague**.

He was survived by his father, Joshua (Joseph), an oysterman, his mother, Sadie, and a brother, Joseph, and was buried in the Andrews and Daisey Cemetery in Chincoteague.

Alonza Bradley - Alonza was a 49-year-old oysterman who had lived at 235 Main Street in **Chincoteague**. He had been First Mate on the Lightship Winter Quarter before moving to Baltimore for work. Very soon after the move, he died of Influenza on **October 7th**, leaving his wife, Mary, and two children. He was buried in Mechanics Cemetery in Chincoteague.

John Wilson Mumford - John was a 38-year-old fisherman for the Whealton fish Company. The family lived on **Assateague Island**. He was taken ill on October 4th and was under the care of Doctor Smith when he died on **October 7th** of Pneumonia following Influenza. He was survived by his wife and two children and was buried in Mechanics Cemetery in Chincoteague.

Joseph Davis* - Joseph was a 30-year-old, unmarried laborer, born in Ohio but living in **Capeville**, when he fell ill with the flu on October 1st. He was seen by Doctor Gilmer on October 2nd and died on **October 8th** of Bronchial Pneumonia and Influenza. He was buried in the African Baptist Church Cemetery in Cheriton.

Florence Virginia Murray - Florence was the four-year-old daughter of Joseph and Catherine Murray. She was taken ill with the flu and was under the care of Doctor Burwell from October 7th until she died of Influenza on **October 9th**. The family lived "Up the Neck" in **Chincoteague,** where her father was a farmer.

She was survived by her parents, Joseph P. Murray and Catherine Jester Murray, and a sister, Katherine. Her grandfather, Ananias Murray died the following week in Bishopville, Maryland. He may have also been a flu victim. She was probably buried in Red Men's Cemetery in Chincoteague where her parents are buried but there is no cemetery name on the death certificate.

Louisa (Lula) Cutler Rew - Lula was 39 years old, married to her husband, Maurice, living in **Hallwood,** when she was stricken with the flu. She was under the care of Doctor Vadin from October 8th until **October 9th** when she died of Broncho Pneumonia following Influenza.

In addition to her husband, she was survived by at least one child, a daughter, Mabel, who was 11 years old. She was buried in Greenwood Cemetery in Temperanceville.

Corbin Stewart Drummond - Corbin was 37 years old, a married carpenter, living in **Sanford,** but working in Newport News. Together with his wife, Ceasy, they had daughters, Lottie and Nevline. He fell ill with the flu and was under the care of Doctor Fletcher from October 8th until **October 10th** when he died of Pneumonia following Influenza. He was buried in Feddeman Cemetery in Sanford.

Premier Felton* - Premier was a 15-year-old laborer, living in **Keller.** He had not been seen by a doctor when he died of Broncho Pneumonia following Influenza on **October 10th**. He was survived by his father, Joe, and was buried in Red Hill Cemetery in Accomac.

William Savage* - William was the one-year-old son of Lorenzo (Pet), a farm laborer and Nora Savage when he took ill with the flu on September 30th. He was under the care of Doctor Kellam until he died of Pneumonia following Influenza on **October 10th**. The family lived in **Daugherty**. He was survived by his parents and was buried in Graysville Cemetery in Tasley.

William Mapp* - William was a 39-year-old, married, sawmill hand, working for George Jarvis in **Jamesville**. He came down with the flu and was under the care of Doctor Sturgis from October 5th until **October 10th** when he died of Pneumonia following Influenza. He was buried in Occohannock Cemetery in Belle Haven.

Robert Franklin Bull - Robert was a 27-year-old railroad car repair man from **Sanford,** who was working in the Cape Charles Railroad yard. He was under the care of Doctor Fletcher from October 1st until **October 11th** when he died of Pneumonia following Influenza. He was survived by his wife Nona, his parents and four brothers. He was buried in Downings Cemetery in Oak Hall.

Edward James Furniss - Edward was a 25-year-old, married clammer living in **Saxis.** He came down with the flu and was under the care of Doctor Fletcher from October 1st until **October 11th** when he died of Pneumonia following Influenza.

In addition to his wife, he was survived by his parents and many brothers and sisters and was buried in the Baptist Churchyard Cemetery in Saxis.

Harry Absolom Phipps - Harry, age 30, was a well-respected and popular railroad freight agent, when he came down with the flu on October 6th. He was under the care of Doctor Burwell when he died of Lobar Pneumonia following Influenza on **October 11th**.

He was married to Theresa, and they had two daughters, Emma and Mary, and a son, Harry. They lived at 215 Church Street in **Chincoteague.** He was also survived by his parents Emory and Jane. He was buried in Mechanics Cemetery in Chincoteague.

Virginia A. Moore - Virginia was the one-year-old daughter of Rufus Allen and Diena (Laura) Moore of **Cape Charles.** She was seen by Doctor Lum on **October 11th**, the day she died from Broncho Pneumonia following Influenza.

In addition to her parents, she was survived by at least three siblings and was buried in Cape Charles Cemetery.

John Henry Harmon* - John was a 34-year-old, married farmer, living in **Keller,** with his wife, Elishia. He was under the care of Doctor Kellam from October 10th until **October 12th** when he died of Pneumonia following Influenza. He was buried in St. Luke's AME Church Cemetery in Daugherty.

Virgie Mason and unborn child* - Virgie was a 24-year-old woman, married to Isaiah Mason, a farmer, in **Onley.** She came down with the flu in her last months of pregnancy. She was under the care of Doctor Kellam from October 7th until **October 12th** when she died of Double Pneumonia. The baby was lost.

She was survived by her husband and three children and was buried in Metompkin Baptist Church Cemetery in Parksley.

Severin Paul Babin - Severin was a 24-year-old Apprentice Seaman in the United States Naval Reserve Force. He was a native of Louisiana but stationed at Cherrystone Naval Base in **Cape Charles**. He came down with the flu and was under the care of Doctor Spillane from October 5th until **October 12th** when he died of Lobar Pneumonia following Influenza.

He had attended the State Normal School and been a schoolteacher for five years before he enlisted in the Navy. He was survived by his parents and seven brothers and sisters. His body was returned to his hometown of Duplessis, Louisiana for funeral and burial took place in the Catholic Cemetery in Prairieville, Louisiana.

William J. Bibbins* - William was a 30-year-old, married farmer, living near **Exmore**. He was under the care of Doctor Downing from October 10th until **October 12th** when he died of Asthma and Influenza.

He was survived by his wife, Sarah, parents, Peter and Mollie, and seven brothers and sisters and was buried in the Franktown Cemetery, Franktown.

Melnyda A. Milligan - Melnyda was a married, 55-year-old milliner with two sons who lived with her husband, Carl, in **Cape Charles**. She came down with the flu and was under the care of Doctor Lynch from October 4th until **October 12th** when she died of Bronchopneumonia following "Spanish Influenza". She was buried in Cape Charles Cemetery.

James Herbert Ward - James was a 33-year-old married farmer living in **Willis Wharf** when he fell ill with the flu. He was under the care of Doctor Kellam from October 8th until **October 12th** when he died of Bronchopneumonia following Influenza. He was survived by his wife, Addie, and daughters, Beatrice and Belford, and was buried in the Red Bank Baptist Church Cemetery in Marionville.

Mary Ethel Harmon* - Mary was only three months old when she died of the flu. She was the daughter of William Henry Harmon, a farm laborer who worked for Garland Belote. Her mother was Georgie Thompson Harmon. She had been under the care of Doctor Kellam from October 6 until she died on **October 13th**. She was survived by her parents. The family lived in **Onley**. She was buried in St. Luke's AME Church Cemetery in Daugherty.

Margaret E. Whealton Bishop - Margaret was 61 years old when she fell ill with the flu on October 12th in **Chincoteague**. She died on **October 13th**. She was the daughter of the late Joshua Whealton and Nancy Ferguson where the family lived "Up the Neck" in Chincoteague. She was survived by one son and four daughters and was buried in Mechanics Cemetery in Chincoteague.

Lula Parks - Lula was 34 years old and married to Herbert H. Parks living in **Pastoria** (near Parksley). She fell ill with the flu and was under the care of Doctor DeCormis from October 6th until she died on **October 13th** of Influenza and the effects of Nephritis.

She was survived by her husband, one son and three daughters and was buried in Parksley Cemetery.

Lennie White - Lennie was a 25-year-old married housewife, living near **Assawoman**. She came down with the flu and was under Doctor Fletcher's care from October 11th until she died on **October 14th** of Pneumonia following Influenza.

She was survived by her husband, Royal Fletcher White, and sons, William and Carlton, four-year-old twins, and Marvin who was seven months old. She was buried in Hall Cemetery in Messongo.

Lula May Kellam* - Lula was the one-year-old daughter of Richard, a farm laborer, and Rhinie Kellam of **Eastville**. She came down with the flu and was under the care of Doctor Dalby from October 9th until **October 14th** when she died of Influenza.

She was survived by her parents, seven brothers and sisters and was buried in the Bethel Baptist Church Cemetery in Eastville.

Colie Sydney Hutchinson - Colie was a 16-year-old clerk when he fell sick with the flu. He was under the care of Doctor Kellam from October12th until **October 16th** when he died. He was the son of Colie, a house carpenter, and Jennie Hutchinson of **Harborton** near

Pungoteague. He was also survived by brothers, Roger and Colie, and sisters, Virginia and Ida. He was buried in Mount Holly Cemetery in Onancock.

Rhoda (Rita) Laws* - Rhoda was a 14-year-old schoolgirl, daughter of John and Maggie Laws of **Metompkin.** She fell ill with the flu and was under the care of Doctor Kerns from October 15th until **October 17th**, when she died of Bronchial Pneumonia following Influenza.

She was survived by her parents and five brothers and sisters and was buried in First Baptist Church Cemetery in Mappsville.

Ella D. (Elodie) Lynch Russell - Elodie was a 20-year-old clerk "Up the Neck" in **Chincoteague**, when she fell ill with the flu. She was under the care of Doctor Smith from October 10th, until dying of pneumonia following Influenza on **October 17th**.

She was the daughter of Ebba Lynch, a boatman, and Matilda Jester. She was also survived by her husband Allen Russell, three brothers and two sisters, and was buried in Daisey Memorial Cemetery in Chincoteague.

Susan Galena Russell - Glena, a 25-year-old housewife, living in **Chincoteague**, on Clark Street. She was taken ill with the flu and was under the care of Doctor Smith from October 10th until she died on **October 17th**.

She was survived by her husband, Aaron Clayton Russell, a self-employed fisherman, a son, Louis, and daughters Mary, and 6-week-old Elizabeth. She was buried in Mechanics Cemetery in Chincoteague.

Annie Elizabeth Tolbert - Annie was a 21-year-old housewife in **Chincoteague**, who died of Bronchopneumonia following Influenza on **October 17th** after a short illness. She had been under the care of Doctor Burwell.

She was survived by her husband, Allen, one child, and parents, William Chandler and Sadie Birch Chandler. She was buried in Mechanics Cemetery in Chincoteague.

John Winifred Drummond* - John was the four-month-old son of Emma Drummond and Benjamin Jacobs of **Onancock**. He came down with the flu and was under the care of Doctor Powell from October 15th until **October 18th** when he died of Pneumonia following Influenza. He was survived by his parents and was buried in Joynes Cemetery in Onancock.

Abbit Chester Pettit* - Abbit was a 25-year-old farmer, living with his wife, Beatrice, and son Chester in **Daugherty**. He fell ill with the flu and was under the care of Doctor DeCormis from October 6th until **October 18th** when he died of Pneumonia following Influenza.

He was survived by his wife and son. Another son, Joseph, was born three months after his death. He was buried in Metompkin Cemetery.

Thomas Stephen Pettit - Thomas was a 32-year-old merchant living in **Silva,** when he came down with the flu. He was under the care of Doctor Dickerson from October 9th until **October 18th** when he died of Pneumonia following Influenza.

He was survived by his parents Samuel and Sarah Petitt, and was buried in Silva, at a private residence.

Charles Taylor Ruffin* - Charles was a 23-year-old married laborer, living in **Daugherty**. He became ill with the flu and was under the care of Doctor Kellam from October 1st until **October 18th** when he died of Pneumonia.

He was survived by his wife and four children and was buried in St. Luke's AME Church Cemetery in Daugherty.

Eva Crosley* - Eva was 23 years old and living in **Melfa** with her mother. She did not have any medical care when she died on **October 19th** of Influenza.

She was survived by her mother, Maggie Crosley, and her father Fred Justice, and was buried in Joynes Cemetery in Onancock.

Mildred W. Oldrich - Mildred was a married 21-year-old when she came down with the flu on October 14th and died on **October 20th** of Influenza complicated by gastritis.

She was survived by her husband, who may have been Herman Oldrich. He opened a bakery in Chincoteague in 1916. She was also survived by her parents. Oliver Logan and Rebecca Booth Wimbrow who lived in **Chincoteague**. She was buried in Mechanics Cemetery in Chincoteague.

Garland Beach Downing - Garland, a 24-year-old bank clerk in Newport News, came down with the flu on October 10th and died on **October 20th**. He was from **Keller** and had only recently moved to the mainland for work.

He was survived by his wife and two children, his parents and a brother and sister. He was buried in the Downing Burial Ground in Wachapreague.

Naomi Laws* - Naomi was the 9-month-old daughter of Lewis, a farmer, and Clementine Laws of **Mappsville**. She became sick with the Flu and was under the care of Doctor Kerns from October 10th until **October 20th** when she died of Bronchial Pneumonia following Influenza.

She was survived by her parents and several brothers and sisters and was buried in the First Baptist Church Cemetery in Mappsville.

Henry Thomas Taylor* - Henry was a 42-year-old farm laborer, married to Sarah and living in **Oak Hall**. He fell sick with the flu and was under the care of Doctor Matthews from October 8th until **October 20th** when he died of Lobar Pneumonia following Influenza.

He was survived by his wife Sarah, and several sons and daughters. After his death, Sarah cared for her children by taking in washing. He was buried in the Friendship United Methodist Church Cemetery in Wattsville.

Willie Wright Wessells - Willie was a 38-year-old housewife from **Parksley**, when she fell ill with the flu. She was under the care of Doctor Drummond from October 10th until she died on **October 20th** of Pneumonia following Influenza.

She was survived by Roy, her husband, and three children, Jewell, Preston, and Carroll and was buried in Parksley Cemetery.

Bessie Veney* - Bessie was 11 years old, living with her father George and mother, Sadie near **Pungoteague**. She came down with the flu and was under the care of Doctor Mears from October 18h until she died on **October 20th**. She was buried in Bacon Hill Cemetery in Exmore.

Alonzo Eugene Matthews - Alonzo was a 19-year-old fisherman living in **Saxis**, when he was taken ill with the flu on October 10th. He was under the care of Doctor Fletcher until he died on **October 20th** of Pneumonia following Influenza.

He was survived by his parents, two brothers and two sisters. He was buried in St. Paul's Cemetery, Marion Station, Maryland.

Hampton Dennis* - Hampton was a 32-year-old, single, farm laborer, living with his mother, Sarah Dennis, in **Metompkin**. He already had asthma when he fell ill with the flu. He was under the care of Doctor Parks from October 19th until **October 21st** when he died of Pneumonia following Influenza. He was buried in Metompkin Baptist Church Cemetery in Parksley.

Bertha Lee Dix* - Bertha was the one-year-old daughter of William, a farmer, and Emma Dix of **Metompkin.** She had only been seen by Doctor Harper once when she died on **October 21st** of "Spanish Influenza".

She was survived by her parents and several brothers and sisters and was buried in the Metompkin Baptist Church Cemetery.

Bertie Lee Stirms* - Bertie was only one year old. She was seen by Doctor Cosby on the day she died of Pneumonia following Influenza on **October 21st**. The family lived near **Wachapreague**. She was survived by her parents, George and Emma Stirms, and was buried in Wachapreague Cemetery.

Addie Virginia Lewis - Addie was a 36-year-old housewife in **Hunting Creek**, when she came down with the flu on October 13th and was under the care of Doctor Kerns until **October 21st** when she died of Flu followed by Broncho Pneumonia.

She was the daughter of Wesley and Jennie Lewis and was survived by her husband, Samuel, and four children and was buried in Hunting Creek Cemetery.

Edward Wilkins* - Edward was the 6-month-old son of Annie Wilkins and Edward Purnell of **Eastville**. He was only seen by Doctor Fields on the day of his death of Acute Catarrhal Pneumonia following Influenza on **October 21st**. He was buried in the Bethel African American Methodist Episcopal Church Cemetery in Eastville.

Earnest P. Marshall - Earnest was a 36-year-old Oysterman in the **Atlantic Magisterial District,** when he fell ill with the flu. He was under the care of Doctor Fletcher from October 10th until **October 22nd** when he died of Pneumonia following Influenza.

He was survived by his wife, Senie, and daughter Helen. However, Senie died in January of 1919 of Typhoid fever, leaving 12-year-old Helen an orphan. They are both buried in the Baptist Church Cemetery in Saxis.

Gay Patterson Somers - Gay was a 20-year-old, native of **Bloxom**, and was visiting Lynchburg, in October when the flu broke out in that city. She volunteered to care for the sick and became infected on October 9th. She died on **October 20th**.

Her funeral was conducted by the Reverend R. S. Monds whose 17-year-old son, Cecil, had been one of the first to die in the epidemic a few weeks earlier. Gay was survived by her parents, one sister and three brothers. She was buried in the Parksley Cemetery.

Arinthia E. Walker - Arinthia was the 6-month-old daughter of Roland, a farmer, and Lula Walker who lived in **Lee Mont,** (near Parksley). She had only been seen once by Doctor Fletcher before she died on **October 23rd** of Meningitis following Influenza. She was survived by her parents and many stepbrothers and sisters and was buried in Parksley Cemetery.

Lorenzo and Mary Elizabeth Wilson* - Lorenzo was a 28-year-old farmer, married to Maggie, with five children, living in **Bloxom**. Mary Elizabeth was their 20-month-old daughter. Mary Elizabeth caught the flu and was under the care of Doctor Kerns from

October 10th until **October 17th** when she died of Bronchial Pneumonia following Influenza. Lorenzo was under the care of Doctor Kerns from October 19th until **October 23rd** when he also died of Bronchial Pneumonia following Influenza. They were buried in Bloxom, possibly in the Macedonia Baptist Church Cemetery.

Marita E. Wise* - Marita was the two-year-old daughter of John and Mattie Wise of **Onancock**. She fell ill with the flu and was under the care of Doctor West from October 15th until **October 23rd** when she died of Bronchopneumonia following Influenza. She was buried in the Joynes Burial Ground in Onancock.

Charlie and Pearl Garrison Collins* - Charlie was the son of Lewis and Pearl Collins of **Exmore**. Pearl, 25 years old, came down with the flu first and was under the care of Doctor Mears from October 20th until **October 27th** when she died of Lobar Pneumonia following Influenza. Charlie came down with the Flu and was seen by Doctor Mears, but he died nine weeks short of his first birthday on **October 23rd** of Bronchopneumonia following Influenza. They were both buried in a Northampton County Cemetery.

Lewis Collins later remarried and had a long life with many children.

Eunace Frances Taylor* - Eunace was the 20-year-old daughter of Thomas and Mary Taylor of **Wattsville**. She was under the care of Doctor Lankford from October 20th until **October 24th** when she died of Pneumonia complicated by Pregnancy following Influenza. She was buried in Friendship United Methodist Cemetery in Wattsville.

Edward Thomas (Drummond) Parker* - Edward was a 34-year-old, unmarried, farm laborer, son of Ada Drummond and Savage Crippen of **Onancock**. He may have also used Drummond as his last name. He was under the care of Doctor Powell from October 21st until **October 25th** when he died of Pneumonia following Influenza. He was buried in the Bayside Community Cemetery in Onancock.

Pearl Lee Onley and Baby Onley - Pearl was 33 years old, married to Jeter Onley, a carpenter in a shipyard, and living in **Cape Charles**. She came down with the flu and was under the care of Doctor Lynch from October 14th. She was six and a half months pregnant and gave birth prematurely to a baby girl on **October 25th**. The baby only lived a short time and Doctor Lynch attributed the premature birth to Pearl's Influenza.

Pearl died of Bronchopneumonia following Influenza on **October 29th**. She was survived by her husband and three children and she and the baby were buried in Groton Cemetery, Hallwood.

Jesse Bonnewell - Jesse was a 17-year-old Railroad agent in **Bloxom**, when he contracted the flu. He was under the care of Doctor Kerns from October 15th to **October 25th** when he died.

He was survived by his parents, J. W. and Mary, and several brothers and sisters. He was buried in Bloxom Cemetery.

William Travis - William was a 19-year-old Piler on a steamer from **Capeville**, when he became sick with the flu. He was under the care of Doctor Vader from October 14th, until he died 11 days later on **October 25th** of Pneumonia following Influenza.

He was the son of Thomas, an oysterman, and Neena Mears Travis. He was buried in a Capeville Methodist Church Cemetery.

William Tankard Belote - William (Tank) was a 32-year-old farmer in **Painter**, when he was taken ill with the flu. He was under the care of Doctor Cash from October 19th until he died eight days later on **October 27th** of Double Pneumonia following Influenza.

He was survived by his wife, Fannie, his mother, three sisters and two brothers. He was buried in Onancock Cemetery.

Stanley Lee Stran* - Stanley was the one-year-old son of John, a farmer, and Cordelia Stran of Melfa. He was under the care of Doctor West for only two days when he died of Bronchopneumonia on October 27th.

He was survived by his parents, two brothers and a sister and was buried in the Red Hill Cemetery in Accomac.

Southey Goffigon* - Southey was a 34-year-old, married Dock Laborer, living in **Cheriton**, when he fell ill with the flu. He was under the care of Doctor Fields from October 13th until he died on **October 28th** of Bronchopneumonia following "Spanish Influenza".

He was the son of John and Tabitha Goffigon and was survived by his wife, Maud. He was buried in the African Baptist Church Cemetery in Cheriton.

George Cubler* - George was a 36-year-old, married laborer in **Onancock.** He was under the care of Doctor Powell from October 16th until **October 29th** when he died of Broncho Pneumonia following Influenza. He was buried in Onancock in an unknown cemetery.

Harry Earl Dise - Harry was the five-year-old son of Isaac, a Waterman, and Brasora Dise of **Tangier Island.** He was under the care of Doctor Gladstone for only two days when he died of Double Lobar Pneumonia likely following Influenza on **October 29th**. He was buried in a unknown cemetery on Tangier Island.

Willie J. Trader* - Willie was the two-year-old son of John and Amanda Trader in the **Lee Magisterial District**. He was under the care of Doctor Fletcher from October 27th until **October 29th** when he died of Pneumonia following Influenza. He was buried in Accomack County in an unknown cemetery.

Lenora Bunting* - Lenora was 21 years old and married to Charles Bunting, a Barrel Cooper, living in **Painter,** when she contracted the flu. She was under the care of Doctor Cosby from October 15th until **October 30th** when she died of Broncho Pneumonia following Influenza.

She was the daughter of John and Haster Sample and was survived by her husband. She was buried in the New Mount Zion Baptist Church Cemetery in Painter.

Clarence Elton Burch - Clarence was a 36-year-old graduate of Washington and Lee University and worked as the Adams Express

Agent in **Chincoteague** when he was taken ill with the flu on October 21st. He died on **October 28th**.

He was survived by his wife, Mary, and five children. He was buried in an unknown cemetery in Chincoteague.

Emma Custis* - Emma was a divorced mother of two who worked as a Washerwoman in **Onancock**. She was under the care of Doctor Burwell from October 21st until **October 28th** when she died of Lobar Pneumonia following Influenza.

She was survived by her daughter Annie, 11, and son, Robert 14 and was buried in an unknown cemetery in Chincoteague.

Samuel Elton Shields* - Samuel was the three-month-old son of Samuel, a farm laborer, and Rena Shields of **Daugherty**. He was under the care of Doctor DeCormis for only two days when he died of Influenza on **October 28th**. He was buried in St. Luke's AME Church Cemetery in Daugherty.

Seymour Lewis Savage Jr.* - Seymour was a married man of 28 working as a laborer at the East Package Company in **Exmore** when he contracted the flu. He had no medical care when he died on **October 30th**, the cause of death was Influenza.

He was the son of Seymour and Eddie Savage and was survived by his wife, Ada, and daughter, Theresa. He was buried at the Ebenezer Baptist Church Cemetery in Wardtown.

Southey Bingham* - Southey was 89 years old, widowed laborer, living in **Eastville** when he came down with the flu. He was under the care of Doctor Walker from October 20th until **October 31st** when he died of Lobar Pneumonia following Influenza.

He was survived by his children, Joseph, Amelia, Maria, and Severn and was buried in the Bethel Baptist Church Cemetery in Eastville.

Chapter 3 – It Burns
November 1918

Doctor Oscar Littleton Powell was born in 1875 in Onancock and attended the Margaret and Onancock Academies. He went on to Harvard University and then Jefferson Medical College in Philadelphia where he graduated in the class of 1900.

He returned to practice medicine in Onancock for 25 years and died in 1925 at the age of 50 after a long illness. Doctor Powell lost the first of nine patients to the Flu in November.

Officials scaled back prevention precautions thinking the epidemic had peaked. The Board of Health of Accomack County cancelled the order to close stores, barber shops, moving picture shows and other public meeting places. Closing schools was left to local authorities and churches were advised to follow the advice of local physicians. There were 38 deaths in November.

> **BOARD OF HEALTH NOTICE**
>
> The epidemic of Influenza in Accomack County having to a great extent declined, notice is hereby given that the restrictions as to closing stores, barber shops and moving picture halls, and other public meeting places is therefore cancelled as of this date, November 1st, 1918.
>
> The request to close churches is likewise withdrawn, outside of the incorporated limits of the town of Onancock. Local conditions will control the latter places, and the ministers are requested to follow the advice of the physicians of that town. Schools will be opened or closed according to the best judgment of the trustees of the respective districts.
>
> J. W. Bowdoin,
> J. H. Ayres,
> R. J. White,
> O. R. Fletcher,
> Board of Health.

Peninsula Enterprise 2 November 1918

Charles Anderton Grace Westcott - Charles was 17 years old and a crew member on a light ship when he came down with the flu. He was under the care of Doctor Holland from October 27th until **November 1st** when he died of Pneumonia following Influenza.

His family had moved to **Chincoteague** in 1905 when his father, Walter, became Assistant Keeper of the lighthouse. Charles was survived by his parents, Walter and Elizabeth, and several brothers and sisters. He was buried in Mechanics Cemetery in Chincoteague.

Samuel Taylor* - Samuel was a 17-year-old farmer living in **Oak Hall,** with his parents. He was under the care of Doctor Matthews from October 10th until **November 1st** when he died of the complications of Influenza.

He was survived by his parents, Henry Taylor and Sarah Benson Taylor, and several brothers and sisters and was buried in Downing's Cemetery in Oak Hall.

Margaret Moore - Margaret Moore was three years old and the daughter of Ernest and Ella Moore in **Eastville** when she came down with the flu on October 15th. She was under the care of Doctor Holland from October 15th until she died on **November 1st** of Bronchial Pneumonia following Influenza. She was buried in the Eastville Baptist Church Cemetery.

William Henderson Eskridge - William was the three-year-old, first-born son of John, a Waterman, and Alice Eskridge of **Tangier**. He was under the care of Doctor Gladstone from late October until **November 4th** when he died of Double Broncho Pneumonia following Influenza.

He was survived by his parents and was buried in an unknown cemetery on Tangier Island.

Mary Sample* - Mary was a 38-year-old, married, domestic living in **Pungoteague**. She was under the care of Doctor White from October 20th until **November 4th** when she died of Broncho Pneumonia following Influenza.

She was survived by her mother, Ellen Harris, and was buried in the Red Hill Cemetery in Accomac.

Magaline Ayres* - Magaline was the 12th of 13 children of Thomas and Lottie Ayres, living near **Onley**. She came down with the flu and was under the care of Doctor Kellam from October 23rd and died on **November 1st** of Influenza. She was buried in a cemetery in Onancock.

Pearl Mears Bundick - Pearl was 21 years old, living in **Quinby**, with her husband, Luther when she contracted the flu. She was under the care of Doctor Cosby from October 27th until she died on **November 1st** from influenza following childbirth.

She was survived by her husband, parents, Andrew and Amanda, and a sister, Ethel. She was buried in Quinby Cemetery.

Edwin Johnson Crockett - Edwin was the first child born to Walton Edwin Crockett and Lena Johnson who lived on **Tangier Island.** He was only 10 months old when he contracted the flu on October 27th. He died on **November 5th** and was buried in an unknown cemetery on Tangier Island. He was survived by his parents.

Minnie and George Maynard Poulson* - Minnie Topping Poulson was 26 years old, married to George and living in **Onley**. She was under the care of Doctor Kellam from November 2nd until **November 6th** when she died of Pneumonia following influenza which was complicated by a miscarriage.

Her eight-year-old son George also was ill with the flu and under Doctor Kellam's care from November 2nd and died on **November 5th**. They are both buried in the Savageville Cemetery in Onancock.

Lusetta Taylor* - Lusetta was the 10-year-old daughter of Thomas and Mary Taylor of **Wattsville**. She was seen by Doctor Matthews on November 3rd and died on **November 5th** of Influenza. She was buried in Friendship United Methodist Church Cemetery in Wattsville.

William Milton Ayres* - William was a 28-year-old farm laborer in or near **Painter**. He was under the care of Doctor West when he died of Lobar Pneumonia following Influenza on **November 6th**.

He was survived by his wife, Louisa, son, Thomas, mother, Mary, and eight brothers and sisters. He was buried in Mt. Zion Baptist Church cemetery in Painter.

Robert Van Dike Collins* - Robert was only 10 months old when Doctor Downing was called to his home. Unfortunately, by the time Doctor Downing arrived on **November 6th**, Robert had died of Pneumonia following Influenza.

He was the son of Caleb Collins. His mother's name cannot be read clearly on the death certificate, bur appears to be Lee Upshur. He was buried in the New Allen Memorial AME Church Cemetery in **Franktown**.

Carrie Hall* - Carrie was a 25-year-old housewife in **Willis Wharf** when she contracted the flu. She died on **November 6th**. She was the daughter of Jim and Mattie Walker and was buried in an unknown cemetery in Exmore.

James Henry and Bertha Tyler* - James and Bertha were mother and son. James was eight years old in **Onancock** when he fell ill with the flu. He was under the care of Doctor Powell from October 27th until **November 7th** when he died. He was the son of Oscar and Bertha Tyler. He was also survived by four brothers and sisters.

Bertha was 27 years old when she died two days after James on **November 9th**. They were buried in Joynes Burial Ground in Onancock, two days apart.

Elton Lee and Elizah Cropper* - Elton was a 23-year-old laborer living in **Wattsville**, when he contracted the flu. He was under Doctor Vaden's care for four days until he died on **November 8th**. His parents were Nathan and Martha Cropper.

Elizah was Nathan's one-year old sister. She also died of the flu on **November 11th**.

They were survived by their parents and many brothers and sisters and were buried in the Friendship United Methodist Church Cemetery in Wattsville.

Joshua David Malone - Joshua was a 35-year-old, married farmer living near **Wattsville**, when Doctor Matthews first called to treat him for influenza on November 2nd. He died on **November 9th** of Pneumonia following Influenza.

He was survived by his wife, Cora, daughter, Katherine, as well as his parents, three sisters and five brothers. He was buried in the Brittingham Cemetery which may be known today as the Nelson Cemetery on Route 13 at the Maryland/Virginia State line.

Mary Ellen Boyer* - Mary was 10 days short of a year old when she came down with the flu. Her parents, William and Sarah had only recently moved to **Bayview**, from New York. She was first seen by Doctor York on November 6 but died on **November 10th** of "Broncho Pneumonia following Influenza".

She was buried in the African Baptist Church Cemetery in Cheriton.

John Thomas Collins* - John was the 12-year-old son of John H. and Emma Savage Collins. He was under the care of Doctor Downing from October 31st until November 11th when he died of Pneumonia following Influenza. The family lived in **Exmore** at the time of his death where his father was a farm laborer. He was survived by his parents and brothers and sisters and was buried in the New Allen Memorial AME Church Cemetery in Franktown.

Lafayette Robins - Lafayette was a 45-year-old, married, Captain of a schooner from **Jamesville**, when he came down with the flu. He was attended by Doctor Sturgis from October 12th until **November 12th** when he died of Pneumonia following Influenza.

He was the son of Lafayette Robins Sr, and Susan Robins and was buried in Phillips Place near Belle Haven.

Charles Laurel Parks - Charles was the first-born son of William and Edna Parks of **Tangier Island** and he was the Master of a fishing boat. Influenza came to their home on the Main Ridge on October 30th. Charles was under the care of Doctor Gladstone from October 30th until he died of Pneumonia following Influenza on **November 12th**.

Charles was survived by his parents and two older sisters, Ila, and Margaret. He was laid to rest in an unknown cemetery on Tangier Island.

Eva May White - Eva was 18 and had married her husband, Hiram in **Chincoteague** shortly after he was inducted into the Army in 1917. In May of 1918 their son, Thomas Edward, was born. Doctor Bell treated Eva for the flu from October 31st until her death on **November 13th** of Broncho Pneumonia. She was buried in Red Men's Cemetery in Chincoteague.

Clara May Dise - Clara was the unmarried 27-year-old daughter of John, a fisherman, and Julia Dise living on **Tangier Island**. She was treated by Doctor Gladstone from October 31st until her death on **November 15th**. In addition to her parents, she was survived by two sisters and a brother. She was buried in an unknown cemetery on Tangier Island.

Mamie Dennis Trader* - Mamie was 21 years old, married to Charlie Trader and living in **Onancock**. She was under the care of Doctor Powell from November 7th until **November 16th** when she died of Broncho Pneumonia. She was the daughter of Mr. Northam and Sallie Dennis and was buried in Joynes Cemetery in Onancock.

Marian Townsend* - Marian was the seven-year-old, only daughter of John Henry Townsend and Nollie Fisher Townsend, who were married in Chincoteague on January 25, 1913. John was a Waterman and the family lived in **Greenbackville**.
Marian came down with the flu and was cared for by Doctor Dickerson until her death on **November 17th**. She was survived by her parents, John, and Nila Fisher Townsend, and was buried in Tabernacle Baptist Church Cemetery in Horntown.

Ruth Hall Wise* - Ruth was 31 years old and married to Thomas Isaiah Wise, a truck Farmer in **Onancock**. They had been married 10 years when Ruth fell ill with the Flu. She was cared for by Doctor Fosque until her death on **November 20th**. She was survived by her husband, two daughters and two sons and was buried in Bayside Cemetery in Onancock.

Eunice Evans* - Eunice was the three-year-old daughter of Lunnie and Olie Evans who lived in the **Atlantic** Magisterial District. Eunice was attended to by Doctor Alva Matthews on November 19th, but she died soon after on **November 21st**. She was buried in Byrd's Cemetery in Mears Station.

Susan Rebecca Robbins - Susan was a 24-year-old married housewife, eight months pregnant, living near **Bird's Nest** with her husband, Henry, a farm laborer, when she contracted the flu. She was under the care of Doctor Jackson from **November 15th** until November 20th when she died of Influenza complicated by her pregnancy. She was buried in the Red Bank Baptist Church Cemetery in Marionville.

Anna Laura Nordstrom - Anna was 32 years old, married to John and mother of five children living near **Bird's Nest** when she contracted the flu. She was under the care of Doctor Kellam from November 19th until **November 20th** when she died of Bronchopneumonia following Influenza. Her parents were Orbi Downing and Ester Hudson Downing. She was buried in the Red Bank Baptist Church Cemetery in Marionville.

Laura Copes* - Laura was the 19-year-old daughter of John and Sallie Cropper Dennis. She was married but we do not have her husband's name. They lived in the **Lee** Magisterial District when she fell ill with the Flu. She was under the care of Doctor Powell from November 7th till **November 21st** when she died of Bronchopneumonia complicated by Influenza. She was buried in Joynes Cemetery.

Nat Howard* - Nat was only one month old when she came down with the flu. She was under the care of Doctor Powell from November 18th until **November 21st** when she died of Broncho Pneumonia following Influenza. She was the daughter of Mamie Trader and Charlie Trader who lived in the **Lee Magisterial District** of Accomack County and was buried in Joynes Cemetery.

Alfred Wilson Parks - Alfred was the first born, two-year-old son of Clayton and Emma Parks of **Tangier Island**. He was treated for the Flu by Doctor Gladstone from November 4th till **November 21st** when he died of Pleuro Pneumonia following Influenza. He was buried on an unknown cemetery on Tangier Island.

Norman R. Allen* - Norman was the 18-year-old son of Will Logan and Berlina Allen of the **Lee** Magisterial District of Accomack County. He was a farm laborer and was under the care of Doctor DeCormis for the Flu and Diphtheria from November 7th until **November 22nd** when he died. He was buried in Graysville Cemetery in Tasley.

Emma Logan, Elton Logan and Auedta Palmer* - Emma Lottie Logan was a 35-year-old wife and mother of five in **Chincoteague**. Her husband, George, was an Oysterman and they lived on the Second Ridge up in the Woods according to the 1910 census. She was seen by Doctor White only on the day she died of Pneumonia following Influenza, on **November 27th**.

Auedta Palmer was the 21-year-old, married daughter of Emma and George Logan. She was seen by Doctor White on November 27th and died the next day on **November 28th** of Pneumonia following Influenza.

Elton Logan was the 12-year-old son of George and Emma Logan. Elton came down with the Flu on November 28th when his mother Emma and sister, Auedta, had died from the Flu. He lived until **December 4th** when he died of Pneumonia following Influenza.

George Logan lost his wife and two children to the Flu epidemic. No further record of the family turns up in census records. They are buried in an unknown cemetery on Chincoteague Island.

Chapter 4 – Holiday Grief
December 1918

Bertram Hensel Gilmer was born in 1874 in Richmond. He came to the Eastern Shore with his wife, Violet, and was practicing medicine in the Capeville District at his home on Seaside County Road but by 1917 had moved to Cape Charles and was at 227 Randolph Avenue. During the flu epidemic, he cared for many patients, nine of whom died. He died in 1922 when he was 47 years old while visiting Richmond and was buried in the Cape Charles Cemetery.

December saw an increase in deaths as the virus found new victims. 47 people died during this holiday month.

> Our school has been ordered closed by the Board of Health, owing to the outbreak of the influenza, as there are several cases reported in town.

Peninsula Enterprise 7 December 1918 - Keller

> **ONLEY**
>
> Mr. Clarence Revell has moved to Cheriton.
>
> Mrs. Mollie Mears is the guest of her brother, Mr. Milton Byrd.
>
> The Onley High School has been closed on account of the influenza.

Peninsula Enterprise 14 December 1918 – Onley

> Our town has been recently visited by an epidemic of Spanish influenza, one hundred or more of its citizens having been stricken with it, two cases resulting fatally.

Peninsula Enterprise 21 December 1918 - Wachapreague

Clifford Arrington Nottingham - Clifford was a 38-year-old farmer, married father of three sons living on Cape Charles Road in **Cape Charles** when he contracted the flu. He was under the care of Doctor Gilmer from November 20th until **December 1st** when he died of Lobar Pneumonia following Influenza.

He was survived by his wife, Nettie, sons Roy, John and Clifford and his parents George and Eleanor Nottingham. He was buried in Cape Charles Cemetery.

Colie Harmon Jr.* - Colie was the four-month-old son of Colie Harmon Sr., a farmer, and his wife Carrie, living in **Jamesville**. There was no doctor caring for him when he died on **December 1st** of Influenza. He was buried in the Ebenezer Baptist Church Cemetery in Wardtown on December 2nd. He was survived by his parents and two siblings.

Stanley Joynes Marsh - Stanley was 21 months old when he came down with the flu. He was the 2nd child of Lewis, the Manager of a roads machine, and Annie Marsh of **Onancock**.

Doctor Fosque cared for him from November 27th until **December 2nd** when he died of Pneumonia following Influenza. In addition to his parents, he was survived by his brother, Lewis. He was buried in Mt. Holly Cemetery in Onancock.

Sallie S. Isdell - Sallie was 33 years old, married to John Isdell, a Waterman, and living in **Bird's Nest**. She came down with the flu and was under the care of Doctor Downing from November 23rd until **December 2nd** when she died of Pneumonia following Influenza. She was buried in the Red Bank Baptist Church Cemetery in Marionville.

Cole E. James - Cole was the 27-year-old, unmarried daughter of Jesse James and Lizzie Carey James. The family lived in **Capeville**. She was under the care of Doctor Gilmer from November 28th till **December 4th** when she died of Broncho Pneumonia following Spanish Influenza. She was buried in Cape Charles Cemetery.

Leonard Joseph Stevens - Leonard was a 22-year-old, unmarried Oysterman living in **Pungoteague** and was the 3rd son of the five children of Joe and Mollie Stephens. He was under the care of Doctor

White from November 30th until **December 5th** when he died of Broncho Pneumonia following Influenza. He was buried in Wachapreague Cemetery.

Eva May, Marris Louise, Hershel James and Infant Boy Tallifarro* (This name may also be Tolever) - Eva was the 27-year-old wife of Hershel James Toliver, an Oysterman, living near Bellestown. She contracted the Flu and was under the care of Doctor Mears from December 2nd until **December 9th** when she died of Pneumonia following Influenzas.

Marris Louise was her three-year-old daughter who also contracted the Flu and died of Pneumonia following Influenza on the same day as her mother, December 9th.

Hershel James was her two-year-old son who died on **December 10th** of the Bronchopneumonia following Influenza.

Also lost to the family was a one-month-old boy who died on **December 8th**.

They were survived by husband, Hershel, and also three other children. They were buried in Bacon (Baken) Hill Cemetery in Exmore. Their records are interesting because there are duplicate death certificates under the name Tallifarro and Toliver.

Robert Leslie Sacks - Robert was the 21-year-old son of Max and Ada Sacks. They were Russian Jewish immigrants who settled in **Birds Nest**. Max was a merchant in the dry good business and had a store, possibly in Cape Charles.

Robert Sacks with his parents at about age 12
Courtesy of Michael Hyman

Robert contracted the flu and was under Doctor White's care from December 5th to **December 9th** when he died.

He was survived by his parents and brother, Louis, and sister, Ida.

He was buried in the Beth Yehuda-Anshe Kurland Congregational Cemetery in Baltimore, Maryland.

Washington Hunt - Washington was an 83-year-old farmer living on Bayside County Road in **Capeville** when he was taken ill with the Flu. He was under the care of Doctor Lynch from December 1st until **December 10th** when he died of Broncho Pneumonia following "Spanish Influenza". His wife, Lucy, had died in 1898 but together they had over a dozen children. He was buried in the "Old Homestead" in Capeville.

Elton Heath Belote - Elton was a 29-year-old clerk in **Onancock**, living with his wife of eight years, Amanda, and his six-year-old son, William, when he contracted the Flu. He was under the care of Doctor Mason from December 2nd until **December 10th**, when he died from Double Lobar Pneumonia and Influenza with Mitral Insufficiency as a contributing factor. He was buried in Onancock Cemetery.

Georgie T. Phillips - Georgie was the 30-year-old wife of Brooks Phillips, a Waterman and mother of two in **Pungoteague**. She came down with the Flu and was under Doctor Kellam's care from December 1st until December 10th when she died of Influenza, Pneumonia and Childbirth. No record of the child was recorded. She was survived by her husband, Brooks, and a daughter, Elsie, and a son, Brooks, and was buried in Wachapreague Cemetery.

Bessie Anna Taylor - Bessie was a 27-year-old housewife from **Capeville,** married to Clarence Taylor and the mother of a two-year-old boy, Melvin. She came down with the Flu and was under the care of Doctor Gilmer from December 3rd till **December 11th** when she died of Lobar Pneumonia following Spanish Influenza. She was buried in the Cape Charles Cemetery.

Eunice Parks - Eunice was the 17-year-old daughter of Thomas, a farmer, and Arinthia Parks of **Justicesville**. She came down with the Flu and was under the care of Doctor Drummond from December 6th until **December 12th** when she died of Broncho Pneumonia following Influenza. She was survived by her parents and older brothers Charles and Grover. A younger sister, Bernice, had died in 1911 at two years of age. Eunice was buried in Liberty Cemetery in Parksley.

Charles Chaplin Drummond* - Charles was a 28-year-old laborer married to his wife, Rosetta, in the Lee Magisterial District of Accomack County. He was taken ill with the Flu and was under the care of Doctor DeCormis from November 29th until **December 13th** when he died of Pneumonia following Influenza. He was survived by his wife and three children and was buried in St. Luke's Cemetery.

Elizabeth Smith* - Elizabeth was the three-month-old daughter of Henry and Malinda Smith of **Eastville**. Elizabeth was their only child and took ill with the Flu and had no medical care before she died on **December 15th** of Influenza. She was buried in the Union Baptist Church Cemetery.

Herbert Burton Parsons - Herbert was the eight-year-old son of William and Helen Burton Parsons of **Onley**. He was under the care of Doctor Kellam from December 5th until **December 15th** when he died of Pneumonia following Influenza. He was survived by his parents, brother, William, and grandparents. He was buried in Edge Hill Cemetery.

Edith Mae Beatty - Edith was 37 years old and married to Roland Beatty, a Railroad Clerk, living in **Cape Charles**. They were originally from Altoona, Pennsylvania but had moved to Cape Charles for Roland's job with the Railroad.

Edith came down with the Flu and was under the care of Doctor Lum from December 13th until **December 17th** when she died of Lobar Pneumonia following Spanish Influenza. She was survived by Roland and their children, Elizabeth, Kenneth, and Catherine. She was buried in her hometown of Altoona, Pennsylvania.

Lula V. Jester - Lula was the 20-year-old daughter of William and Laura Jester of **Chincoteague,** living at 24 Main Street. She was under the care of Doctor Bell from December 9th until **December 17th** when she died of Broncho Pneumonia "supposed to have followed Influenza".

She was survived by her parents, brothers, Walter and Harry, and sister, Gladys, and was buried in Greenwood Cemetery in Chincoteague.

Claud J. Matthews - Claud was the 31-year-old son of Ambrose Frank Matthews, the Mayor of **Chincoteague,** and Catherine M. Babbitt Matthews. He had been elected Cashier of the Farmers and

Merchants Bank of New Church and served in that position before enlisting in the Naval Reserve.

He was under the care of Doctor Emory Bell from December 11th till **December 17th** when he died of Pneumonia following Influenza. He was survived by his parents and brother, Charles, and sister, Gladys. He was buried in the Nelson Cemetery in New Church.

Lillie Margaret Howard - Lillie was the 27-year-old wife of Ernest Howard, a Railroad signal maintenance worker in **Eastville**. They were both born in Maryland.

Lille came down with the Flu and was under the care of a doctor from December 14th till **December 18th** when she died of Lobular Pneumonia following Influenza. She was survived by her husband Earnest and also a son, James, and was buried in the Bethany United Methodist Church Cemetery in Pocomoke, Maryland.

Rosena Mabel Willis* - Rosena was the 28-year-old wife of Otha Willis and mother of two children living in **Eastville**, working as a dressmaker. She was under the care of Doctor Reid from December 8th till **December 18th** when she died of Lobar Pneumonia following Influenza. She was buried in the Wallace Burial Ground; the location is unknown.

Carlton John Culver - Carlton was a 28-year-old Railroad Yard Conductor living in the **Capeville** Magisterial District and probably worked at the Cape Charles Railroad yard. He was born in Sussex, Delaware and had come to Cape Charles sometime after 1910 to work.

He was married to Helen and together they had two sons, George and Raymond, when he fell ill with the Flu. He was under the care of Doctor Gilmer from December 15th until **December 19th** when he died of Lobar Pneumonia following Influenza. He was buried in St. Stephen's Cemetery in Delmar, Delaware.

Mamie Beckett* - Mamie was a 36-year-old housewife living in the **Lee Magisterial District**. She was under the care of Doctor Kellam from December 18th until **December 20th** when she died.

Doctor Kellam listed her cause of death as Influenza – Childbirth. There is no name for her husband or child in the records. She was buried in the Savageville Cemetery in Onancock.

Mary C. Andrews - Mary was 43 years old and married to George Andrews, an Oysterman, for 22 years, living in **Chincoteague** at 326 Main Street. They had nine child, Rebecca, who was 17 when her mother came down with the Flu. Mary was under the care of Doctor White from December 6th until **December 19th** when she died. She was also survived by her father, Joseph and several sisters and brothers and was buried in Andrews Daisey Cemetery in Chincoteague.

Grover C. Smith - Grover was the 16-year-old son of Edgar, a laborer, and Ida Smith of **Chincoteague**. He took ill with the Flu and was under the care of Doctor Bell from December 12th until **December 20th** when he died of Bronchial Pneumonia following the "Spanish Influenza". He was buried in an unknown cemetery in Chincoteague.

Elijah Thomas Trader* - Elijah was a six-year-old schoolboy and son of Joel, a Day Worker, and Charlotte Trader of **Horntown**. He was under the care of Doctor John Dickerson from December 19th until **December 21st** when he died of Lobar Pneumonia "supposed to have followed Influenza". He was survived by his parents and his two-year-old brother, Elton, and was buried in an unknown cemetery in Horntown.

Albert Brown* - Albert was an 11-year-old schoolboy and the son of James Brown, a laborer, and Laura Smith, a laundress of **Eastville Station**. He came down with the Flu and was under the care of Doctor Walker from December 18th until **December 22nd** when he died of Lobar Pneumonia following Spanish Influenza. He was buried in the Ebenezer AME Church Cemetery in Cape Charles.

Thomas Spence - Thomas was a 35-year-old, married Oysterman from **Quinby**. He came down with the Flu and was under the care of Doctor White from December 20th to **December 22nd** when he died of Broncho Pneumonia following Influenza. He was buried in an unknown cemetery in Quinby.

Nannie Louise Bowden - Nannie was the daughter of Aaron, an Oysterman, and Nannie Bowden of **Chincoteague**. She was only one year old when she contracted the Flu. She was under the care of Doctor White for 10 days until she died on **December 24th**, Christmas Eve, of Pneumonia. She was survived by five brothers and sisters and was buried in an unknown cemetery in Chincoteague.

Beulah Roberts* - Beulah was the six-month-old daughter of Lee, a Farmer, and Letitia Savage who lived in the **Lee Magisterial District** of Accomack County. She contracted the Flu and was under the care of Doctor DeCormis from December 20th until **December 24th**, Christmas Eve, when she died of Pneumonia following Influenza. She was survived by her parents and two brothers and was buried in Graysville Cemetery in Tasley.

Helena Savage* - Helena was the 37-year-old wife of George Savage, a Farmer, of **Franktown**. She was under the care of Doctor Reid from December 21st until **December 25**, when she died of Pneumonia following Influenza on Christmas Day. She was buried in an unknown cemetery near Franktown.

Emma Lottie Hatton* - Emma was a 27-year-old married woman in **Pungoteague** when she came down with the Flu. She was under the care of Doctor West from December 16th until **December 25th** when she died on Christmas Day of Lobar Pneumonia following Influenza. She was survived by her husband, John, and two sons and was buried in Holy Trinity Baptist Cemetery in Painter.

Joseph Kellam - Joseph was a single, 50-year-old farm laborer from **Pungoteague**. He was under the care of Doctor Cosby from December 19th until **December 26th** when he died of Pneumonia following Influenza. He was survived by his father, Shadrack and brother, William and was buried in Saint George's Episcopal Church Cemetery in Pungoteague.

Lee Hurley - Lee was the 33-year-old farmer, husband of Naomi (Onie) Hurley, and father to a number of children in **New Church**. He was under the care of Doctor Fletcher from December 20th until

December 27th when he died of Bronchial Pneumonia following Influenza. He was survived by his wife, children, and parents, Henry, and Julia. He was buried in the Salem Methodist Church Cemetery in Pocomoke, Maryland.

Oscar Rally Ward - Oscar was a 25year old, married farmer, living in **Exmore**. He was under the care of Doctor Hyslup from December 15th until **December 26th** when he died of Pneumonia following Influenza.

He was survived by his wife, Lillie, and two children and was buried in the Franktown Cemetery,

John William Kelley - John was a 46-year-old farmer, married to Evelyn with eight children, living in **New Church**. He was under the care of Doctor Matthews from December 8th until **December 27th** when he died of Bronchial Pneumonia following Influenza. He was also survived by three sisters and his burial was in Downings Cemetery in Oak Hall.

Adolphus Douglas* - Adolphus was just 11 months old when he died of Bronchial Pneumonia following Influenza on **December 28th** while under the care of Doctor Kerns. He was the son of James Henry Douglas and Emma Fletcher Douglas of **Temperanceville**. His burial location is identified as "Head of Neck" on the death certificate.

Ella Frances Mapp* - Ella was almost two months old, the daughter of Edward, a farmer, and Amelia Mapp of **Pungoteague** when she contracted the Flu. She was seen by Doctor West but died the following day, **December 28th** of Influenza. Her burial place is not known.

Garland Otho White - Garland was a 20-year-old, unmarried Machinist working at the Onancock Machine Works and living in **Onancock**. He was under the care of Doctor Robertson from December 17th until **December 28th** when he died from Influenza complicated by Double Pneumonia.

He was survived by his parents, Otho and Sudie, and a sister, Minnie, and brothers, Thomas and Timothy, and was buried in Onancock Cemetery. His brother, Timothy, later died of the flu on **January 29th**, 1919.

Arinthia Joynes Custis* - Arinthia was a 56-year-old widow of Henry Custis from **Eastville**. She had given birth to six children over the years of her marriage to Henry, but only two sons survived at the time of her death. She had been under the care of Doctor Fields since December 21st but died on **December 29th** of "Spanish Influenza". She was survived by her sons, William and Edward Custis, and was buried in the Ebenezer AME Church Cemetery in Cape Charles.

Norman Fields* - Norman was a 23-year-old farm laborer, living with his wife, Marie, and two sons in the **Atlantic Magisterial District** on Wallops Neck Road. He came down with the Flu and was under the care of Doctor Fletcher until **December 30th** when he died of Pneumonia following Influenza. He was survived by his wife and sons, Norman and John, and was buried in Friendship United Methodist Episcopal Church Cemetery in Wattsville.

Alpha Omega Doughty* - Alpha (Alphie) was the 28-year-old wife of George, a Cooper at a barrel factory, and mother of two in **Franktown**. She was under the care of Doctor Fletcher from December 26th until **December 30th** when she died of Pneumonia following Influenza. She was survived by her husband and daughters, Flossie and Milon, and was buried in an unknown cemetery in Northampton County.

George Elton Major* - George was barely nine years old, living with his mother, Minnie, and father, George, a Truck Farmer, in **Nandua**. He contracted the Flu and was under the care of Doctor West for only a day when he died of Lobar Pneumonia following Influenza on **December 31st**. He was survived by his parents and sisters Fannie, Anna and Ella. His final resting place is not known.

George S. Mears* - George was a 34-year-old truck farmer, unmarried, and living in **Painter** when he fell ill with the flu. He was under Doctor Cosby's care from December 24th until **December 31st**

when he died of Lobar Pneumonia following Influenza. He was buried in Belle Haven Cemetery.

Chapter 5 – Beginning of the End
January 1919

Doctor Alva Adair Matthews was born in 1884 and grew up in Accomack County where his father had found work with the Commission of Fisheries. He was a 1910 graduate of the University of Maryland School of Medicine in Baltimore, He practiced medicine in Oak Hall. Nine of his patients died of the Flu during the pandemic..

On January 4th, the Peninsula Enterprise announced that Influenza was still prevalent in New Church. On January 11th, the Painter High School was closed due to Influenza and on January 18th, Chincoteague announced that it was free of the flu and the school was open. 31 new victims will die this month. It is the first month to see a decline in fatalities since the second surge in December.

> **NEW CHURCH**
> Influenza is still prevalent in our community.
> Misses Cecil Paradee and Ella John-

Peninsula Enterprise 4 January 1919 - New Church

> The High School has been closed at this place, until further orders. One of our teachers is quite sick with the "Flu."

Peninsula Enterprise 11 January 1919 – Painter

> Our school opened Monday with a good attendance. We are glad to report that we have no influenza in our town.

Peninsula Enterprise 18 January 1919 - Chincoteague

Elnoria Downing* - Elnoria was almost three years old, the daughter of Matthew, a farmer, and Bertie Downing, living in **Wattsville**. She was under the care of Doctor Fletcher from January 4th until **January 9th** when she died of Pneumonia following Influenza. She was survived by her parents and was buried in a "burying ground near Wattsville".

Carrie and James Manning - James was a druggist from Portsmouth, and he met and married Carrie Nock of **Assawoman**, in June of 1915. They made their home in Portsmouth but came to spend the holidays with the Nock family in December of 1918. Carrie came down with the Flu and Doctor Matthews made his first call on December 29th. On January 2nd, he began treatment of James as well. James died at 6 AM on **January 6th**. Carrie followed him at 9 PM that night.

They were survived by their son James and daughter, Ruth. James was buried in the Oak Grove Cemetery in Portsmouth while Carrie was laid to rest in the Assawoman Methodist Church Cemetery.

Lizzie Susan Bundick* - Lizzie was the daughter of Alfred, a farmer, and Susan Bundick of **Franktown**. She was under the care of Doctor Reid from December 23rd until **January 7th**, one day after her 17th birthday, when she died of Lobar Pneumonia following Influenza. She was survived by her parents and many brothers and sisters and was buried in an unknown cemetery near Exmore.

Annie Eliza Davis - Annie was 66 years old, the wife of Mordecai (Major) T. Davis, a farmer living in **Wattsville**. She was under the care of Doctor Vaden from January 5th until **January 7th** when she died of Bronchial Pneumonia following Influenza. She was survived by her husband and children and was buried in Nelson Cemetery in New Church.

Melicia Frances Hudson* - Melicia was the 10-month-old daughter of Charles and Jennie Hudson of **Wattsville.** She was under the care of Doctor Graden when she died of Broncho Pneumonia following Influenza on **January 7th**. She was buried in the Friendship United Methodist Church Cemetery in Wattsville.

Mary Elizabeth Northam Hall - Mary was 82 years old and the Widow of Cephas Corbin Hall of **Atlantic.** She was under the care of Doctor Fletcher from January 2nd until **January 8th** when she died of Influenza. She was survived by her children and was buried in the Hall Cemetery in Messongo.

Bettie Fitchett* - Bettie was the 53-year-old wife of Minnie Fitchett, a barber, from **Eastville.** Doctor Walker visited her on **January 9th,** but she died shortly thereafter of Acute Lobar Pneumonia following Influenza. She was survived by her husband and was buried in a Methodist Church Cemetery, possibly Bethel AME in Eastville.

Arrena Nock Dennis* - Rena was the 46-year-old wife of Joshua Dennis, a farmer, from **Metompkin.** She was under the care of Doctor Bowdon from January 6th **until January 11th** when she died of Influenza. She was survived by her husband and children from her first marriage to John Watson and was buried in an unknown cemetery in Mappsville.

Eugene Brickhouse* - Eugene was the 12-year-old son of Elton and Fannie Brickhouse of **Exmore.** He was under the care of Doctor Mears from January 10th until **January 15th** when he died of Broncho Pneumonia following Influenza and was buried in the Ebenezer Baptist Church Cemetery in Wardtown.

Purnell Moore* - Purnell Moore was the one-year-old son of Henry and Millie Moore of **Pungoteague.** He did not receive any medical care and died of Influenza on **January15th**. He was buried in Boston Cemetery now Shiloh Baptist Church Cemetery in Pungoteague.

Ella and Charles Upshaw* - Ella, three years old, and Charles, four months old, were the children of David and Mannie Upshaw of

Eastville. They were under the care of Doctor Dalby for Influenza when Charles died on **January 16th** and then Ella died on **January 18th**. They were buried in an unknown cemetery in Bridgetown.

Leroy Sample* - Leroy was the four-year-old, and youngest, son of Major and Laura Sample of Wardtown. He was under the care of Doctor Reid from January 8th until **January 16th** when he died of Pneumonia following Influenza. He was survived by his parents, four sisters and two brothers and was buried in Occohannock Neck.

Allie Milton Stran* - Allie was the one-year-old son of Egwart and Rachel Stran of **Pungoteague.** He did not receive any medical care before he died of Influenza on **January 17th**. He was buried in the Shiloh Baptist Church Cemetery in Boston, Virginia.

Maggie Jane Marshall* - Maggie was the 26-year-old wife of George C. White of **Oak Hall**. George had been married before with children. Maggie and George had been married for five years, with a newborn daughter when she was taken Ill with the Flu. She was under the care of Doctor Matthews from January 14th until **January 19th** when she died of Broncho Pneumonia. She was buried in Wattsville. There is no record of George after her death and their three children then went to live with Maggie's brother and family.

Grover Lee Charnock - Grover was the 17-year-old son of John, an Oysterman, and Mary Charnock of **Tangier Island**. Grover had taken up work as a Waterman when he came down with the Flu. He was under the care of Doctor Gladstone from January 7th until **January 19th** when he died of Pneumonia following Influenza. He was survived by his parents, four brothers and two sisters and was buried on an unknown cemetery on Tangier Island.

Mary Ann Martin - Mary was the 28-year-old wife of William Hyslop of **Croddockville.** They had been married six years, with two daughters when Mary came down with the flu. She was cared for by Doctor John Hyslop from January 14th until **January 21st** when she died of Pneumonia following Influenza. She was buried in Belle Haven Cemetery.

Queenie, Minnie, and Arthur (Hopsie) Booker* - Queenie and Arthur (Hopsie) Booker Sr. had been married 15 years and had eight children. They lived in Seaview, near **Capeville,** where Hopsie was a farm laborer. Influenza came to their home on January 14th when Doctor Fields began treatment of two-month-old daughter, Minnie. Eight days later on **January 22nd** she died of Acute Bronchopneumonia.

Two-year-old Hopsie Jr. was next, and he died on **January 25th**. Their mother, 30-year-old Queenie, died on **January 29th** of Lobar Pneumonia.

They were survived by Hopsie Sr. and Ellen, Augustus, Janie, Grace, Queenie, and Kemper. They were buried in Northampton County, possibly in the First Baptist Church-Capeville Cemetery near Dalbys.

Rayman Holdman* - Rayman was the 11-year-old son of Joseph and Lillie Holdman of the Capeville Magisterial District, probably near **Dalbys**. He was under the care of Doctor Gilmer from January 19th until **January 23rd** when he died of Bronchopneumonia following Influenza. He was buried in the African Baptist Church Cemetery in Cheriton.

Jacob Sheppard* - Jacob was the 24-year-old farm laborer in **Wardtown**, and son of Servern Sheppard and Sarah Trower. He came down with the Flu and was under the care of Doctor Nash from January 21st until **January 24th** when he died of Lobar Pneumonia following Influenza. He was buried in a cemetery in Wardtown.

Charlotte Alice Gladding - Alice was the 62-year-old daughter of John and Margaret Gladding of **Horntown**. She was under the care of Doctor Dickerson from January 15th until **January 24th** when she died of Broncho Pneumonia following Influenza. She was buried in the family burying ground in Miona.

Olevia May Steelman - Olevia was the 34-year-old wife of Nathaniel Steelman, an Oysterman, living in **Chincoteague**. She was born in Maryland and was visiting her family when she came down with the Flu. She died on **January 27th** in her home in Chincoteague. She was survived by her husband, her parents and five brothers and was buried in Greenwood Cemetery in Chincoteague.

Maurice Clark* - Maurice was the 6-month-old son of John Clark and Topsy Foster where they lived in the **Capeville** area. He died of the Flu with no medical care on **January 28th** and was buried in the African Baptist Church Cemetery in Cheriton.

Margaret and Ione Scott - Margaret was the two-year-old daughter of William, a farmer, and Ione Scott in the **Capeville** area. Ione was 25 years old and was the first to get the Flu. She was under the care of Doctor Gilmer from January 22nd until **January 29th** when she died of Lobar Pneumonia, along with her unborn baby.

Margaret was under Doctor Gilmer's care from January 25th until **January 30th** when she died of Broncho Pneumonia. They are both buried in the Cape Charles Cemetery.

Allie Smith* - Allie was the 28-year-old wife of Frank Smith of **Capeville**. She had no medical care until Doctor Vaden saw her on **January 29th** when she died of Bronchopneumonia following Influenza. She was buried in the Capeville First Baptist Church Cemetery.

Timothy Robert White - Robert, his preferred name, was a married truck farmer in **Onancock**, when he came down with the Flu. He was under the care of Doctor Lofland from January 20th until **January 29th** when he died of Lobar Pneumonia following the Spanish Flu. He was survived by his wife, Mary, his parents, and a sister. His brother, Garland, had died of the flu on December 28th. He was buried in Onancock Cemetery.

Fannie Thomas Bell - Fannie was a married 36-year-old housewife from the **Eastville** area. She was under the care of Doctor Sturgis from January 18th until **January 30th** when she died of Pneumonia following Influenza. She was buried in the Red Bank Baptist Church Cemetery, Marionville.

Chapter 6 – The Cool Down
February 1919

Doctor Robert W. White was a native of Delaware and the son of Doctor Henry White of Wilmington. He attended Delaware Collage (University of Delaware) and graduated from Jefferson Medical College in Philadelphia. He practiced medicine in Chincoteague, for over 35 years, from his home at 61 South Main Street where he lived with his family. He died at home in Chincoteague in 1925 at the age of 73.

There were only 9 deaths this month as the epidemic wound down.

Capeville

There is still sum flu around here, but it appears to have almost gone.

Peninsula Enterprise 8 February 1919 - Capeville

Precilla Spady* - Precilla was the 17-year-old daughter of Samuel, a farmer, and Sarah Spady of **Capeville.** She was under the care of Doctor Lynch from January 15th until **February 5th** when she died of Bronchopneumonia following Influenza.

She was survived by her parents, five sisters and one brother and was buried in the African Methodist Episcopal Church Cemetery in Capeville.

Thomas C. Carpenter - Thomas was a 48-year-old Oysterman, married to his wife, Lizzie, for 22 years from **Chincoteague.** They lived at 305 Pension Street with their three children when he came down with the Flu. He was under the care of Doctor White from February 2nd until **February 10th** when he died of Pneumonia following Influenza. He was survived by his wife and son, Harvey, and daughter, Minnie, and was buried in Mechanics Cemetery in Chincoteague.

John Robertson* - John was a 35-year-old auto mechanic, married to Annie in **Cape Charles**. He came down with the Flu and was under the care of Doctor Palmer from January 26th until **February 14th** when he died of Double Pneumonia following Influenza. He was buried in Cape Charles Cemetery.

Minnie Otelia Watson* - Minnie was 11 days old, the daughter of Harry Thomas Watson, a "Shoe Cobbler" and Minnie Moore Watson who lived in **Harborton**. She had received no medical care when she died on **February 14th** of Influenza. She was survived by her parents and at least one sister, Mary Frances, and was buried in Boston Cemetery, now Shiloh Baptist Cemetery, in Pungoteague.

Gladdis Aline Bell - Gladdis was the two-year-old daughter of Alonzo R. and Mary Margaret Kellam Bell of **Onancock**. She became ill with the Flu and was cared for by Doctor Fosque from February 10th until **February 17th** when she died of Pneumonia following Influenza. She was buried in Onancock Cemetery.

Morris Wilson Burton - Morris was the two-month-old son of Harry Floyd Burton, a farmer, and Mary Anne Mears of **Locustville**. He came down with the Flu and was under the care of Doctor Kellam from February 20th until **February 27th** when he died of

Bronchopneumonia following Influenza. He was buried in Mount Holly Cemetery in Onancock.

Margaret Fosque* - Margaret was the 7-month-old daughter of Servus Fosque and Addie May Young of **Accomac**. She came down with the Flu and was under the care of Doctor Ayres from February 18th until **February 25th** when she died of Pneumonia following Influenza. She was buried in Grayville Cemetery.

Ansley Hopkins - Ansley was a 35-year-old cook for the Coast Guard in **Chincoteague**. He came down with the Flu and was under the care of Doctor White from February 19th until **February 22nd** when he died of Pneumonia following Influenza. He was survived by his wife, Ola Beebe Hopkins, and was buried in Greenwood Cemetery in Chincoteague.

Emma Peggy Matthews Mapp - Emma was 67 years old, living in **Bird's Nest**. She had an early marriage to Charles Van Ness but was single at the time of her death. She was under the care of Doctor Jackson from February 12th until **February 24th** when she died of Influenza complicated by Endocarditis. She was buried in the Hungars Episcopal Church Cemetery in Bridgetown.

Chapter 7 – The End
March 1919

Sterling Otelius Fields was a native of Newport News, and a 1912 graduate of the University of Pennsylvania. He was an African American doctor who treated many patients during the epidemic, 12 of whom died of the disease. He was practicing medicine in Cape Charles. His last patient was 6-month-old Lavinia Evans.

The epidemic slowly ended on the Eastern Shore of Virginia with only 6 deaths March. Normalcy soon returned to the shore after the worst epidemic anyone had ever seen.

Charles Thomas Drummond* - Thomas was a 36-year-old, married farmer in **Melfa**. He came down with the Flu and was under the care of Doctor DeCormis from February 22nd until **March 7th** when he died of Lobar Pneumonia following Influenza. He was survived by his wife, Estella Kellam Drummond, and was buried in St. Luke's Cemetery.

Levi N. Cathell - Levi was a 40-year-old, married man working at the Life Saving station in **Chincoteague**. He contracted the Flu and was under the care of Doctor Burwell from January 21st until **March 10th** when he died of Influenza. He was the son of John Cathell and Margaret Thornton Cathell and was survived by his wife, Annie, and was buried in Greenwood Cemetery in Chincoteague.

Lavinia Evans* - Lavinia was the 6-month-old daughter of Willie, a farmer, and Leah Evans of **Cheriton**. She came down with the Flu and was under the care of Doctor Fields from March 12th until **March 18th** when she died of Bronchopneumonia following Influenza. She was survived by her parents and was buried in the African Baptist Church Cemetery in Cheriton.

Helen E. Kellam - Helen was the four-year-old daughter and first child of Upsher Franklin Kellam Sr., a blacksmith with his own shop, and Lizzie Showard Kellam of **Capeville**. She contracted the Flu and was under the care of Doctor Gilmer from March 12th until **March 24th** when she died of Bronchopneumonia following Influenza.

She was survived by her parents and was buried in an unknown cemetery in Painter. Within a few months of her death, her mother, Lizzie, had the first of five additional children. In 1921 they named another of their children, Helen, after their lost daughter.

James William Wall - James was an 86-year-old widower, a machinist born in England and living in **Capeville**. He was under the care of Doctor Lynch from March 5th until **March 24th** when he died of Bronchopneumonia following Influenza.

His wife, Elizabeth Morris Wall, had predeceased him but he was survived by five sons and two daughters and was buried in Cape Charles Cemetery.

Fred S. Kellam - Fred was a 35-year-old, married, self-employed Blacksmith, living in Townsend. He was under the care of Doctor Vaden from March 15th until **March 27th** when he died of Lobar Pneumonia following Influenza.

He was survived by his wife, Minnie, and daughter, Della, and was buried in an unknown cemetery in Capeville.

Appendix I - Methodology

Everything starts with a reliable source of information which in this case was a book titled "From Tears to Memories" by James Waine Carpenter Sr. James took on the task of documenting all of the burials in the cemeteries of Chincoteague. It was a monumental task and gave me a start.

I went through that book and highlighted every record that involved a death in 1918 and 1919. Then I went to Ancestry.com and found a goldmine of information in the death certificates for the Commonwealth of Virginia online in searchable and image form. Those records became the primary source of information. It was possible to search by county and date and then find out the cause of death. I started by searching for all the Chincoteague deaths and began recording them in an Excel spreadsheet.

I use a spreadsheet because it helps to identify patterns and relationships. When I had finished the Chincoteague records it was clear that there were a lot of people who died and at the same time, I knew I was only seeing part of the story. Chincoteague is an island on a peninsula, and they are separate but at the same time connected by commerce and culture. Travel in 1918 was relatively easy and that promoted the spread of disease. I decided to expand the research to the entire Eastern Shore of Virginia which includes both Accomack and Northampton Counties. The death certificates made that possible.

Death Certificates - There are some challenges presented by the death certificates. Doctors handwriting was first among them. Names were often misspelled. Sometimes the age was not known, and the doctor guessed. Many times, the burial location was just the town or even near the town.

I am using the death certificate for Thomas Harman as an example. There is a wealth of information there.

Ancestry.com - All Virginia, U.S., Death Records, 1912-2014

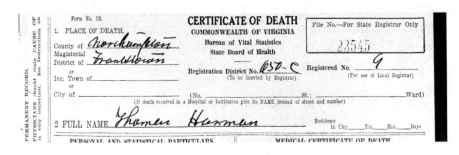

This is one of the more legible examples. The image above is the top section enlarged for readability. His name is fairly clear although this copy has been enhanced. The County is Northampton, and the Magisterial District is Franktown. For many people living outside of towns, that may be the only location for them.

On the left side, he identified as a single, Black male, Laborer, born August 15, 1875. He was 43 years, 1 month and 13 days old at time of death.

He was born in Northampton County. His parents were George Harman and Mary Anne Huling. Note that his mother was the informant, and she was located in Jamesville. That is the clue to where Thomas may have actually lived.

The right side shows the date of death as September 28, 1918. The cause of death is "Pneumonia following Influenza". It is signed by Doctor Reed, but he notes that no doctor was present, and the information was supplied by the informant. The place of burial was Occohannock Cemetery which in Belle Haven.

Using the information extracted from the death certificate, I followed up with a search of the Peninsula Enterprise archive and Ancestry.com to gather as much information as was possible.

Some people had family trees on Ancestry. Others were found in census records and for the men in draft records. Burial records could be found on Findagrave.com. Those sources helped to fill in the spreadsheet. I went on to write a paragraph about each person using that information.

I have no doubt that there are bound to be some errors. There were some people who were very prominent, and the records are lengthy. Many others left little behind in the official record except for a death certificate.

Newspaper Death Notices – Newspapers were very useful but not always accurate. The Peninsula Enterprise was much different than a big city newspaper. In Philadelphia or Richmond, there would be a separate section entirely devoted to death notices. They were listed alphabetically. There might be 100 every day but they were all easy to find.

In the Peninsula Enterprise, death notices were included in an area of local town news that was likely submitted by someone living in each town who reported on local news of all kinds. Deaths would be listed along with other news like births, accidents, sickness, and other gossip. That made it much harder to find them and easy to miss them.

When found, the notices might have also identified someone by their nickname or preferred name rather than their legal name which was on the death certificate. In one case, a child who had died was misidentified by her sister's name who had died years before.

The notices were a valuable resource but could often be inaccurate.

Appendix II – Demographics

Total deaths = 211

104 white
median age of death = 27
Male median age of death = 28
Female median age of death = 27

107 black
median age of death = 14
Male median age of death = 12
Female median age of death = 15

Population Statistics**

Accomack County 34,795
White –21,520 – 62%
Black – 13,213 – 38%
Other - 62

Northampton County 17,852
White - 8,152 – 46%
Black – 9,587 – 54%
Other – 113

Total Eastern Shore – 52,647
White – 29,672 – 56%
Black – 22,800 – 43%
Other - 175

**Fourteenth Census of the United States, State Compendium, Virginia - https://www2.census.gov/prod2/decennial/documents/06229686v44-49ch2.pdf

Appendix III – Alphabetical Index

Name	Page
Allen, Norman R.	44
Andrews, Mary C.	51
Andrews, William E.	22
Ayres, Magaline	39
Ayres, William	39
Babin, Severin Paul	26
Beatty, Edith Mae	49
Beckett, Mammie	50
Bell, Fannie Thomas	62
Bell, Gladis Aline	64
Belote, Elton Heath	48
Belote, William Tankard	34
Bibbins, William J.	26
Bingham, Southey	36
Bishop, Margaret E. Whealton	27
Bonnewell, Jesse S.	34
Booker, Hopsie	60
Booker, Minnie	60
Booker, Queen	60
Bowden, Frisby Rayfield	22
Bowden, Nannie (Nancy) Louise	52
Boyer, Mary Ellen	41
Bradley, Alonza	23
Brickhouse, Eugene	58
Brown, Albert	51
Bull, Robert Franklin	24
Bundick, Lizzie Susan	57
Bundick, Pearl B.	39
Bunting, Lenora	35
Burch, Clarence Elton	35

Burton, Morris Wilson	64
Carpenter, Thomas C.	64
Cathell, Levi N.	67
Charnock, Grover Lee	59
Clark, Maurice	61
Collins, Charlie	33
Collins, John Thomas	41
Collins, Pearl Garrison	33
Collins, Robert Van Dike	40
Copes, Laura	43
Crockett, Edwin Johnson	39
Cropper, Elizah	40
Cropper, Elton Lee	40
Crosley, Eva	29
Cubler, George	35
Culver, Carlton John	50
Custis, Arinthia Joynes	54
Custis, Emma	36
Davis, Annie Eliza	57
Davis, Joseph	23
Davis, Orlin	22
Dennis, Arrena Nock	58
Dennis, Hampton	31
Dise, Clara May	42
Dise, Harry Earl	35
Dix, Bertha Lee	31
Doughty, Alpha (Alfie) Omega	54
Doughty, Ellison Rickets	22
Douglas, Adolphus	53
Downing, Elnoria	57
Downing, Garland Beach	30
Drummond, Charles Chaplin	48
Drummond, Corbin Stewart	24
Drummond, John Winifred	29
Drummond, Charles Thomas	67

Name	Age
Eskridge, William Henderson	38
Evans, Eunice	42
Evans, Luvinia	67
Felton, Premier	24
Fields, Norman R.	54
Fitchett, Bettie	58
Fosque, Margaret	66
Furniss, Edward James	25
Gladding, Charlotte Alice	60
Goffigon, Southey	35
Hall, Carrie	40
Hall, Mary Elizabeth Northam	58
Harman, Thomas	19
Harmon, John Henry	25
Harmon, May Ethel	26
Harmon Jr., Colie	46
Hatton, Emma Lottie	52
Holdman, Raymond	60
Hopkins, Ansley	65
Howard, Lilly May	50
Howard, Nat	43
Hudson, Melecia Francis	58
Hunt, Washington	47
Hurley, Lee	52
Hutchinson, Colie Sydney	27
Isdell, Sallie S.	46
James, Cole E.	46
Jester, Lula V.	49
Johnson, Nettie Thelma	22
Kellam, Fred	68
Kellam, Helen E.	67
Kellam, Joseph	52
Kellam, Lula May	27
Kelley, John William	53
Laws, Naomi	30
Laws, Rhoda (Rita)	28

Lewis, Addie Virginia	31
Logan, Elton	44
Logan, Emma Lottie	44
Major, George Elton	54
Malone, Joshua David	40
Manning, Carrie Nock	57
Manning, James	57
Mapp, Ella Frances	53
Mapp, Louise	19
Mapp, Peggy Emma Matthews	65
Mapp, William	24
Marsh, Stanley Joynes	46
Marshall, Earnest	32
Marshall, Maggie Janes	59
Martin, Mary Ann	59
Mason, Virgie	25
Matthews, Alonzo Eugene	31
Matthews, Claud J.	49
Mears, George S.	54
Milligan, Melnyda A.	26
Monds, Cecil George Washington	19
Moore, Margaret	38
Moore, Purnell	56
Moore, Virginia A.	25
Mumford, John Wilson	23
Murray, Florence Virginia	23
Nordstrom, Anna Laura	43
Nottingham, Clifford Arrington	46
Oldrich, Mildred W.	29
Onley, baby	34
Onley, Pearl Lee	34
Palmer, Auedta	44
Parker, Edward Thomas	33

Name	Age
Parks, Alfred Wilson	43
Parks, Charles Laurel	41
Parks, Eunice	48
Parks, Lula F.	27
Parsons, Herbert Burton	49
Petit, Abbit Chester	29
Pettit, Thomas Stephen	29
Phillips, Georgia T.	48
Phipps, Harry Absolom	25
Poulson, George Maynard	39
Poulson, Minnie	39
Rew, Louisa (Lula)	23
Robbins, Susan Rebecca	43
Roberts, Buelah	52
Robertson, John	64
Robins, Lafayette	41
Ruffin, Charles Taylor	29
Russell, Ella D. Lynch (Elodie)	28
Russell, Glena	28
Sacks, Robert Leslie	47
Sample, Leroy	59
Sample, Mary	38
Savage, Helena	52
Savage, Seymour Lewis	36
Savage, William	24
Scott, Margaret Lone	61
Scott, Margaret Lone	61
Sheppard, Jacob	60
Shields, Samuel Elton	36
Smith, Allie	61
Smith, Elisabeth	49
Smith, Grover C.	51
Somers, Gay Patterson	32
Spady, Precilla	64
Spence, Thomas	51

Steelman, Olivia May (Olevia)	61
Stevens, Leonard Joseph	46
Stirms, Bertie Lee	31
Stran, Allie Milton	59
Stran, Stanley Lee	34
Taliver (Tallifarro), Eva G.	47
Taliver (Tallifarro), Marris Louise	47
Tallifarro, Hershel	47
Tallifarro, Infant	47
Taylor, Bessie Anna	48
Taylor, Eunace Frances	33
Taylor, Henry Thomas	30
Taylor, Lusetta	39
Taylor, Samuel	38
Tolbert, Annie Elizabeth	28
Townsend, Marian	42
Trader, Elijah Thomas	51
Trader, Mamie	42
Trader, Willie J.	35
Travis, William	34
Tyler, Bertha	40
Tyler, James Henry	40
Upshaw, Charles	59
Upshaw, Ella	59
Veney, Bessie	31
Walker, Arinthia E.	32
Wall, James William	67
Ward, James Herbert	26
Ward, Oscar Rally	53
Watson, Minnie Otelia	64
Wessells, Willie Wright	30
Westcott, Charles Anderton Grace	38
White, Eva May	42
White, Garland O.	53

White, Lennie R.	27
White, Timothy Robert	61
Wilkins, Edward	32
Willis, Rosena Mabel	50
Wilson, Lorenzo	32
Wilson, Mary Elizabeth	32
Wise, Marita E.	33
Wise, Ruth A.	42

Appendix IV - Cemetery Index

Cemetery records are taken from the death certificates. Some cemetery names may have changed. Some place names have fallen into disuse. All are in Virginia unless noted.

Altoona, PA	
Rose Hill Cemetery	Beatty, Edith Mae
Accomac	
Edgehill Cemetery	Parsons, Herbert Burton
Red Hill Cemetery	Felton, Premier
	Sample, Mary
	Stran, Stanley Lee
Accomack County	
Unknown Cemetery	Trader, Willie J.
Atlantic	
Assawoman Methodist Church Cemetery	Manning, Carrie Nock
Baltimore, MD	
Beth Yehuda-Anshe Kurland Congregational Cemetery	Sacks, Robert
Belle Haven	
Belle Haven Cemetery	Mapp, Louise
	Martin, Mary
	Mears, George S.
Occohannock Cemetery	Harman, Thomas
	Mapp, William
Occohannock Neck, Cemetery Unknown	Sample, Leroy
Phillips Place, Cemetery Unknown	Robins, Lafayette
Berlin, MD	
Saint Paul United Methodist Church Cemetery	Matthews, Alonzo Eugene
Bloxom	
Bethel Baptist Church Cemetery	Monds, Cecil George Washington
Bloxom Cemetery	Bonnewell, Jesse S.

Unknown Cemetery possibly Macedonia Baptist	Wilson, Lorenzo Wilson, Mary Elizabeth

Boston

Boston Cemetery/Shiloh Baptist Church Cemetery	Moore, Purnell Stran, Allie Milton Watson, Minnie Otelia

Bridgetown

Hungars Episcopal Church Cemetery	Mapp, Peggy Emma Matthews
Unknown Cemetery	Upshaw, Charles Upshaw, Ella

Cape Charles

Cape Charles Cemetery	James, Cole E. Milligan, Melnyda A. Moore, Virginia A. Nottingham, Clifford Arrington Robertson, John Scott, Margaret Lone Scott, Margaret Lone Taylor, Bessie Anna Wall, James William
Ebenezer AME Church Cemetery	Custis, Arinthia Joynes Brown, Albert

Capeville

Capeville Methodist Church Cemetery	Travis, William
Ebenezer AME Church Cemetery	Spady, Precilla
Old Homestead	Hunt, Washington
Unknown Baptist Church Cemetery	Smith, Allie
Unknown Cemetery	Kellam, Fred

Cheriton

African Baptist Church Cemetery	Boyer, Mary Ellen Clark, Maurice Davis, Joseph Evans, Luvinia Goffigon, Southey Holdman, Raymond

Chincoteague

Andrews and Daisey Cemetery	Andrews, Mary C.
	Andrews, William E.
Daisey Cemetery	Lynch, Ella D. (Elodie)
Greenwood Cemetery	Bowden, Frisby Rayfield
	Cathell, Levi N.
	Hopkins, Ansley
	Jester, Lula V.
	Steelman, Olivia May (Olevia)
Mechanics Cemetery	Bishop, Margaret E. Whealton
	Bradley, Alonza
	Carpenter, Thomas C.
	Mumford, John Wilson
	Oldrich, Mildred W.
	Phipps, Harry Absolom
	Russell, Glena
	Tolbert, Annie Elizabeth
	Westcott, Charles Anderton Grace
Red Mens Cemetery	White, Eva May
Unknown Cemetery	Bowden, Nannie (Nancy) Louise
	Burch, Clarence Elton
	Custis, Emma
	Logan, Elton
	Logan, Emma Lottie
	Murray, Florence Virginia
	Palmer, Auedta
	Smith, Grover C.

Dalbys

Family Burying Ground	Booker , Hopsie
	Booker , Minnie
	Booker , Queen

Delmar, DE

St. Stephens Cemetery	Culver, Carlton John

Daugherty

St. Luke's AME Church Cemetery	Drummond, Charles Chaplin
	Drummond, Thomas
	Harmon, John Henry
	Harmon, May Ethel
	Ruffin, Charles Taylor
	Shields, Samuel Elton

Eastville

Bethel AME Church Cemetery	Kellam, Lula May Wilkins, Edward
Eastville Baptist Church Cemetery	Moore, Margaret
Union Baptist Church Cemetery	Bingham, Southey Smith, Elisabeth
Unknown Cemetery - Possibly Bethel AME Church Cemetery in Eastville	Fitchett, Bettie

Exmore

Bacon (Baken) Hill Cemetery	Taliver (Tallifarro), Eva G. Taliver (Tallifarro), Marris Louise Tallifarro, Hershel Tallifarro, Infant Veney, Bessie
Epworth Methodist Church Cemetery	Doughty, Ellison Rickets
Unknown Cemetery	Hall, Carrie
Unknown Cemetery – near Exmore, VA	Bundick, Lizzie Susan

Franktown

Franktown Cemetery	Bibbins, William J. Johnson, Nettie Thelma Ward, Oscar Rally
New Allen Memorial AME Church Cemetery	Collins, John Thomas Collins, Robert Van Dike
Wallace Burying Ground	Willis, Rosena Mabel
Unknown Cemetery	Doughty, Alpha (Alfie) Omega Savage, Helena

Greenbush

Lewis Cemetery Hunting Creek	Lewis, Addie Virginia

Hallwood

Groton Cemetery	Onley, Baby Onley, Pearl Lee

Head of the Neck

Unknown Cemetery - Head of the Neck	Douglas, Adolphus

Horntown

Tabernacle Baptist Church Cemetery Memorials	Townsend, Marian
Unknown Cemetery	Trader, Elijah Thomas

Marionville

Red Bank Baptist Church Cemetery	Bell, Fannie Thomas Isdell, Sallie S. Nordstrom, Anna Laura Robbins, Susan Rebecca Ward, James Herbert

Mappsville

First Baptist Church Cemetery	Laws, Naomi Laws, Rhoda (Rita) Mears Station Byrds Cemetery Evans, Eunice
Unknown Cemetery	Dennis, Arrena Nock

Mesongo

Hall Cemetery	Hall, Mary Elizabeth Northam

Miona

Family Burying Ground	Gladding, Charlotte Alice

New Church

Nelson Cemetery	Davis, Annie Eliza Matthews, Claud J.

Northampton County

Unknown Cemetery	Collins, Charlie Collins, Pearl Garrison
Unknown Cemetery may be Ebenezer Baptist	Harmon Jr., Colie

Oak Hall

Downings Cemetery	Bull, Robert Franklin Kelley, John William Taylor, Samuel

Onancock

Bayside Community Cemetery	Parker, Edward Thomas Wise, Ruth A.
Joynes Cemetery	Ayres, Magaline Copes, Laura

	Crosley, Eva Drummond, John Winifred Howard, Nat Trader, Mamie Tyler, Bertha Tyler, James Henry Wise, Marita E.
Mount Holly Cemetery	Burton, Morris Wilson Hutchinson, Colie Sydney Marsh, Stanley Joynes
Onancock Cemetery	Bell, Gladis Aline Belote, Elton Heath Belote, William Tankard White, Garland O. White, Timothy Robert
Savageville Cemetery	Beckett, Mammie Paulson, George Maynard Poulson, Minnie
Unknown Cemetery	Cubler, George

Painter

Holy Trinity Baptist Church Cemetery	Hatton, Emma Lottie
Mount Zion Baptist Church Cemetery	Ayres, William
New Mount Zion Baptist Church Cemetery	Bunting, Lenora
Unknown Cemetery	Kellam, Helen E.

Parksley

Hall Cemetery	White, Lennie R.
Liberty Cemetery	Parks, Eunice
Metompkin Baptist Church Cemetery	Dennis, Hampton Dix, Bertha Lee Mason, Virgie Petit, Abbit Chester
Parksley Cemetery	Parks, Lula F. Somers, Gay Patterson Walker, Arinthia E. Wessells, Willie Wright

Pokomoke, MD

Bethany United Methodist Church Cemetery	Howard, Lilly May

Salem Methodist Episcopal Church Cemetery	Hurley, Lee

Portsmouth

Oak Grove Cemetery	Manning, James

Prarieville, LA

Ascension Parish Cemetery	Babin, Severin Paul

Pungoteague

Saint George's Episcopal Church Cemetery	Kellam, Joseph

Quinby

Quinby Cemetery	Bundick, Pearl B.
Unknown Cemetery	Spence, Thomas

Sanford

Feddeman Cemetery	Drummond, Corbin Stewart

Saxis

Baptist Churchyard Cemetery	Furniss, Edward James
	Marshall, Earnest

Silva

Grave in the cornfield behind Hallie Pettit's house in Signpost	Pettit, Thomas Stephen

Snow Hill, MD

Whatcoat United Methodist Church Cemetery	Davis, Orlin

Tangier Island

Unknown Cemetery	Charnock, Grover Lee
	Crockett, Edwin Johnson
	Dise, Clara May
	Dise, Harry Earl
	Eskridge, William Henderson
	Parks, Alfred Wilson
	Parks, Charles Laurel

Tasley

Graysville Cemetery	Allen, Norman R.
	Fosque, Margaret
	Roberts, Buelah
	Savage, William

## Temperanceville	
John W. Taylor Cemetery	Rew, Louisa (Lula)
## Wattsville	
Friendship United Methodist Church Cemetery	Cropper, Elizah Cropper, Elton Lee Fields, Norman R. Hudson, Melecia Francis Taylor, Eunace Frances Taylor, Henry Thomas Taylor, Lusetta
Unknown Cemetery	Downing, Elnoria Marshall, Maggie Janes
## Wachapreague	
Downing Burial Ground	Downing, Garland Beach
Wachapreague Cemetery	Phillips, Georgia T. Stevens, Leonard Joseph Stirms, Bertie Lee
## Wardtown	
Ebenezer Baptist Church Cemetery	Brickhouse, Eugene Savage, Seymour Lewis
## Unknown Location	
Brittingham Cemetery or Nelson Cemetery	Malone, Joshua David
Burial by family	Major, George Elton Mapp, Ella Frances
Unknown Cemetery – Possibly Ebenezer	Sheppard, Jacob

Appendix V – Death Notices

Louise Turlington Mapp

Miss Louise Mapp, daughter of Mr. and Mrs. W. B. Mapp, of Mappsburg, Va., died of Spanish influenza at Hollins College, Salem, Va., on Wednesday night, following a short illness. At the time of going to press no arrangements had been made for the funeral.

Peninsula Enterprise 28 September 1918

Cecil George Washington Monds

Mr. Cecil Monds.

Mr. Cecil Monds, son of Rev. R. S. Monds, of Mappsville, Va., died at Forks Union Military Academy, Fork Union, Va., on Monday, September 30th, 1918, following a short illness. He was taken ill with influenza and later pneumonia developed. Death was due, however, to heart failure. Funeral services were held at Bethel Baptist Church, of which he was a member, on Wednesday, conducted by Dr. A. B. Dunaway, assisted by Revs. F. M. Sanford, Richard Lloyd, R. F. Hopkins, E. C. Davis and J. A. Willoughby. Interment was in the family lot at the church. Mr. Monds was very popular with the people of his community. This was evidenced by the large crowd which attended his funeral and by the beautiful flowers sent as a last tribute to him. He is survived by his father and several brothers.

Peninsula Enterprise 5 October 1918

Frisby Ray Bowden

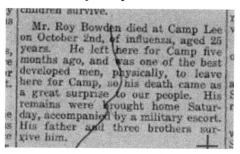

Mr. Roy Bowden died at Camp Lee on October 2nd, of influenza, aged 25 years. He left here for Camp five months ago, and was one of the best developed men, physically, to leave here for Camp, so his death came as a great surprise to our people. His remains were brought home Saturday, accompanied by a military escort. His father and three brothers survive him.

Peninsula Enterprise 12 October 1918

Severin Paul Babin

Severin Paul Babin.

Severin Paul Babin, a young citizen of New River, died at Cherry Stone naval hospital, Cape Charles, Va., on Oct. 12, at the age of 25 years from an atack of influenza. Deceased was a son of Mr. and Mrs. Vincent Babin, of Duplessis. He was born and reared in New River and graduated from the Dutchtown High School, and afterwards taught school for five years. He joined the United States navy on May 5 last, as an apprentice seaman, and was assigned to duty at the naval station at Cape Charles, Va., where he remained up to the time of his death. He was a young man of high character and was honored and respected by all who knew him. The remains were brought to this parish and laid to rest in the Catholic cemetery at Prairieville on Oct. 22, with the funeral rites of the Catholic church.

The Donaldsville Chief 26 October 1918

Orlin Q. Davis

Mr. Olin Davis, the only son of Mr. and Mrs. Quinton Davis, died in Wilmington, Del., on October 3rd, aged 18 years. He was a promising young man and his death was a shock, not only to his family, but to his many friends. He was particularly popular with the younger folks. Burial was at Snow Hill, Md., on Saturday. Besides his parents, he is survived by three sisters, Mrs. W. E. Burton, of Richmond; Mrs. C. P. Custis, of Onancock, and Miss Mildred Davis, of this place.

Peninsula Enterprise 12 October 1918

Ellison Ricketts Doughty

Mr. E. R. Doughty.

Mr. E. R. Doughty, a highly esteemed citizen died at his home at Willis Wharf, last Friday morning of pneumonia, aged about 37 years. Funeral services were held at Broadwater Church Saturday afternoon at 5 o'clock. Interment was made in the church-yard. He is survived by his wife and three small children.

Eastern Shore Herald 12 October 1918

William E. Andrews

Mr. William Andrews, son of Mr. and Mrs. Joseph Andrews, died Monday with the influenza, aged 17 years.

Peninsula Enterprise 12 October 1918

Alonza Bradley

Mr. Alonza Bradley left here a few weeks ago with his family, to work in Baltimore, where he had secured a job. He was taken ill with influenza and died on the 7th inst., after a short illness. His remains were brought here for burial. His wife and two children survive.

Peninsula Enterprise 12 October 1918

John Wilson Mumford

Mr. John Mumford died Monday with the influenza, aged 34 years. He is survived by a wife and three children.

Peninsula Enterprise 12 October 1918

Robert Franklin Bull

DEATHS

Mr. Robert F. Bull

Mr. Robert F. Bull, esteemed and loved by many friends, died at his home at Sanford, Va., on Friday, October 11, 1918 of pneumonia following influenza, after an illness of one week, aged 27 years. He had been a member of Sanford M. E. Church for a number of years, and lived a good and upright life. He was noted for his jolly disposition and kind heart and will be greatly missed by his host of friends. Although we will miss his smiling face from among us, we feel that Robert is safe in the arms of Jesus. His last words were "Father, I am safe around the point."

His heart was pure,
His life was young,
Yet not our will but God's be done.
The brightest, fairest, sweetest flowers
God gathers for His own,
He is happy with the angels
Around our Saviour's throne.

He is survived by his wife, who was the popular Miss Nona McCready, his parents, Mr. and Mrs. Floyd Bull, of Makemie Park, and four brothers, Mr. Finney Bull, of Baltimore, Md., and Messrs. Winfred, Wallace and Richmond Bull, of Makemie Park. Services were held at the grave, conducted by Rev. D. W. Jackson and interment was made in Mulberry Hill Cemetery. The writer and many friends extend their sincere sympathy to the bereaved family.

F.

Peninsula Enterprise 2 November 1918

Harry Absolom Phipps

Mr. Harry Phipps, son of Mr. and Mrs. Emra Phipps, died October 11, of pneumonia, following an attack of influenza, aged 31 years. He had been assistant agent for the P., B. and W. R. R. Co., at this place for a number of years, and was faithful in the performance of his duties. He was courteous and polite and popular with the whole community. He was an upright, honorable, Christian gentleman. He was a member of Accomack Lodge, A. F. and A. M. Besides his parents, he is survived by his wife and three small children.

Peninsula Enterprise 15 October 1918

Melnyda A. Milligan

Mrs. Carl S. Milligan died Saturday morning of pneumonia. She was 65 years of age. Interment was made in Cape Charles cemetery.

Eastern Shore Herald 19 October 1918

James Herbert Ward

Deaths

Mr. James Ward

Mr. James Ward a highly esteemed citizen, died at his home near Willis Wharf, Saturday at 11 o'clock a. m., of influenza, aged about 34 years. Funeral services were held over his remains Monday.

He is survived by his wife and several children.

Eastern Shore Herald 19 October 1918

Margaret E. Whealton Bishop

Mrs. Margaret Bishop died Monday with pneumonia, which developed from influenza, aged sixty years. She is survived by one son, Mr. William Bishop, and four daughters, Mrs. Ella Cropper, of Ocean City; Mrs. Lizzie Lewis, Mrs. Ansel Burch and Mrs. ...attie Kelley, of this place

On Saturday morning, October 12,

Peninsula Enterprise 19 October 1918

Colie Sydney Hutchinson

Harborton was inexpressibly saddened when the news went through town Wednesday morning, October 16th, that Mr. Sydney C. Hutchinson, son of Mr. and Mrs. C. R. Hutchinson, was dead. He was a promising young man, and his death was not only a shock to his family, but to his many friends. He was a very popular young man. It was good to have known him. Many will miss the kindly word and sunny smile. The sympathy of this community goes out to the bereaved ones.

Peninsula Enterprise 19 October 1918

Mildred W. Oldrich

Mrs. Mildred Oldrich died Sunday aged twenty-four years. She is survived by her husband, one child and mother and father, Mr. and Mrs. O. L Wimbrow.

Peninsula Enterprise 26 October 1918

Ella D. (Elodie) Lynch Russell

Mrs. Elodie Russell died Thursday, October 17 with influenza. She is survived by her husband, Mr. Allen Russell.

Peninsula Enterprise 26 October 1918

Susan Galena Russell

Mrs. Aaron Russell died of influenza Friday aged twenty-two years. She is survived by her husband and three children.

Peninsula Enterprise 26 October 1918

Annie Elizabeth Tolbert

Mrs. Annie Tolbert died of influenza last Friday aged twenty years. She leaves her husband, Mr. Allen Tolbert, and one child to mourn her death.

Peninsula Enterprise 26 October 1918

Garland Beach Downing

Mr. Garland Downing

Mr. Garland Downing, formerly of Keller, Va., but recently employed in a bank in Newport News, Va., died in that city of pneumonia on Sunday, October 20th 1918, aged 24 years. After funeral services conducted by Rev. C. H. Kidd at Oak Grove Church on Wednesday, burial was in the family burying ground near Keller, Va. He is survived by his wife and two children, his parents, one sister, Miss Mildred Downing, and a brother, Mr. Dorsey L. Downing.

Peninsula Enterprise 26 Oct 1918

Willie Wright Wessells

settled for the winter.

Mrs. Willie Wright Wessells, wife of Mr. Roy G. Wessells, died at her home near here, last Sunday night, of pneumonia, following an attack of influenza, aged 38 years. Interment was made in Parksley cemetery, Tuesday afternoon, services conducted by her pastor, Rev. E. C. Davis, assisted by the Rev. C. E. Taylor. She was a consistent member of Zion Baptist Church, a woman of good traits and Christian qualities, who will be greatly missed in her home and community. Besides her husband, three children survive, Jewell, Preston and Carroll Wessells.

Peninsula Enterprise 26 October 1918

Alonzo Eugene Matthews

Mr. Alonzo E. Matthews

Mr. Alonzo E. Matthews, son of Mr. and Mrs. W. H. Matthews of Saxis, Va., died at the home of his parents on Sunday, October 20, 1918, after an illness of two weeks of the Spanish influenza and pneumonia. Interment was in St. Paul's Cemetery, Marion Station, Md. Besides his parents he is survived by two brothers, Messrs W. F. and Luther E. Matthews and two sisters, Misses Mary and Grace Matthews.

Peninsula Enterprise 26 October 1918

Addie Virginia Lewis

Mrs. Samuel Lewis.

Mrs. Samuel Lewis, of Hunting Creek, died Monday morning of influenza aged thirty-six years. Funeral services were conducted Tuesday morning by Rev. Howard Link, pastor of the Hunting Creek M. P. Church, of which she was a faithful member and interment was in Liberty cemetery, Parksley, Va. Mrs. Lewis is survived by her husband and four children.

Peninsula Enterprise 26 October 1918

Gay Patterson Somers

Miss Gay Somers.

Miss Gay Somers, daughter of Capt. and Mrs. W. James Somers, of Bloxom, Va., died in a hospital in Lynchburg, Va., on Tuesday of pneumonia, aged 20 years. Miss Somers was visiting in Lynchburg, Va., when the epidemic of influenza broke out. She immediately offered her services in helping to nurse the stricken of that city. She contracted the disease and pneumonia developed. Miss Somers had an attractive personality and a lovely character. There is an old saying "that the good die young" and this would seem very appropriate in the case of this young woman. Her remains were brought to Bloxom and after funeral services conducted by Rev. R. S. Monds her remains were interred in Bloxom Cemetery. She is survived by her parents, one sister, Mrs. Lola Browne, and three brothers, Messrs Grover, Elmer and Chris Somers.

Peninsula Enterprise 26 October 1918

Jesse Bonnewell

Mr. Jesse Bonniville died Thursday night of pneumonia following influenza. He is survived by his parents and several brothers and sisters.

Peninsula Enterprise 2 November 1918

William Tankard Belote

Mr. Tank Beloate, a popular young man and a prosperous farmer of near this place, died at his home on Saturday, October 26th, of influenza followed by pneumonia. Funeral services were conducted at his home on Sunday afternoon by the Rev. C H. Kidd and Rev. J. D. Hosier, of Pungoteague. Interment was in Onancock Cemetery. He is survived by his wife, nee Miss Fannie Sturgis, and mother, Mrs. Emma Beloate; three sisters, Mrs. Will Mears, Mrs. N. H. Gordy, Mrs. Edgar Massey, and two brothers, Messrs. Richard and Clifton Beloate. The pall bearers were: Active, Messrs. Will Phillips, Will Whaley, George Mears, Wm. Sturgis, Will Mears; honorary, Messrs. George Heath, Alden Edmonds, Lynwood Drummond, Early Mears, Will Mears and Upshur Beloate.

Peninsula Enterprise 2 November 1918

Clarence Elton Burch

Mr. C. Elton Burch died October 28, 1918 of influenza, which developed into pneumonia, aged thirty-six years. Mr. Burch attended Washington and Lee University several years. At the time of his death he was the Adams Express agent from this place to Harrington, Del. He was clerk of the town council and an active democrat. He is survived by his widow and five small children.

Peninsula Enterprise 2 November 1918

Charles Anderton Grace Westcott

Mr. Charles Wescott, son of Mr. and Mrs. Walter Wescott, died November 1, 1918, of influenza, aged seventeen years. He is survived by his mother and father.

Peninsula Enterprise 9 November 1918

Pearl Mears Bundick

Mrs. Pearl Mears Bundick died November 1, 1918, of influenza, which developed into pneumonia, aged 21 years. Funeral services were conducted at her home on Saturday morning. Interment was in the cemetery at this place. The deceased is survived by her husband, parents and one sister. She was noted for a kind heart, and will be greatly missed by a host of friends in this community.

Peninsula Enterprise 9 November 1918

Joshua David Malone

Mr. Joshua D. Malone

Mr. Joshua D. Malone died at his home near Wattsville, November 9, 1918, of influenza aged thirty-five years. Funeral services were conducted Sunday, November 11th, by Rev. Thomas C. Jones and interment was in the Brittingham cemetery at the Maryland and Virginia line. Mr. Malone was a member of the Atlantic M. P. Church. He was a prosperous farmer, a kindhearted neighbor and a respected citizen. He is survived by his widow, one child, his parents. Mr. and Mrs. A. T. Malone, three sisters, Mrs. Florence Duffy, Mrs. Mollie Chatam, and Miss Frances Malone and five brothers, Messrs Hartwell M., Roger E., Avery T., Elwood M., and Alex. G. Malone.

Peninsula Enterprise 23 November 1918

Lafayette Robins

Death

Captain Fayette Robins died Nov. 12 after an illness of three weeks, of the Spanish influenza and pneumonia, at his home at James Wharf, aged 45 years. Funeral services were conducted at Bethel M. E. church by Rev. Mr. Moore and burial was made in the family burying ground. Surviving him are his widow and three children, Raymond, Willard and Mrs. Carrie Chandler. Captain Robins was industrious and successful, a fond and indulgent parent and husband and will be greatly missed from his home and community.

Eastern Shore Herald 26 November 1918

Eva May White

Mrs. Eva White died on November 14th, 1918, of influenza, aged nineteen years. She is survived by her husband, Mr. Thomas White, who is in France, and one small child.

Peninsula Enterprise 23 November 1918

Susan Rebecca Robins

Mrs. Sue Robins.

Mrs. Sue Robins, a highly esteemed lady, died at her home near Birds Nest on last Wednesday, aged about 24 years, of influenza. Funeral services were held at Red Bank church Friday afternoon at 3 o'clock, conducted by the pastor, Rev. W. W. Reynolds. Interment in the church yard. She is survived by her husband and two children and several brothers and sisters.

Eastern Shore Herald 30 November 1918

Anna Laura Nordstrom

Mrs. Annie Nordstrum.

Mrs. Annie Nordstrum, wife of Mr. John Nordstrum, died at her home near Birds Nest last Thursday, of Spanish influenza, aged about thirty years. Funeral services were held at Red Bank Baptist church, of which she was a consistent member, Friday afternoon at 3 o'clock, conducted by the pastor, Rev. W. W. Reynolds. Interment in the church yard.

She is survived by her husband and five children.

Eastern Shore Herald 30 November 1918

Clifford Arrington Nottingham

The death of Mr. C. A. Nottingham was quite a shock to our community, having been sick only a few days. The bereaved ones have our sympathy.

Eastern Shore Herald 7 December 1918

Leonard Joseph Stevens

Mr Leonard J. Stevens

Mr. Leonard J. Stevens, a popular and respected young man of Wachapreague, Va., died at his home at that place on Thursday, December 5th, aged 23 years. Death was due to pneumonia. Funeral services were held on Saturday, conducted by Rev. W. C. Jamison and interment was in Wachapreague Cemetery. Surviving him are his parents, Mr. and Mrs. Joe Stevens, two sisters, Misses Blanche and Grace Stevens, and two brothers, Messrs. Upshur and Thompson Stevens.

Peninsula Enterprise 14 December 1918

Washington Hunt

Mr. Washington Hunt.

The funeral of Mr. Washington Hunt who died at his home near Capeville, Tuesday, was held at his late home Wednesday afternoon at 3 o'clock.

The services were conducted by Rev. P. M. Hank, pastor of the Capeville Methodist Church of which Mr. Hunt was a communicant.

In the death of Mr. Hunt Northampton has lost one of her oldest and most respected citizens. He was 83 years old.

He was ever associated with the noblest and best in the community and his integrity, splendid characteristics and genuine culture had endeared him to all who were privileged to know him.

He is survived by eight children---Dr. Washington Hunt, of New York, Mr. Alfred Hunt, of Boston, Mrs. C. W. Cofer, of Smithfield, Mrs. Clifford Goffigon, Mrs. Geo. Tankard, Miss Mary Hunt, and Messrs. Arthur and Herman

Peninsula Enterprise 7 December 1918

Georgie T. Phillips

Mrs. Brooks Phillips.

Mrs. Brooks Phillips died at her home at Wachapreague, Va., Tuesday, December 10th, 1918, of pneumonia, which developed from influenza, aged thirty-three years. Funeral services were conducted on Wednesday by Rev. C. A. Campbell, pastor of the Wachapreague M. E. Church, of which she was a member, and interment was in Wachapreague Cemetery. She is survived by her husband and two children.

Peninsula Enterprise 21 December 1918

Eunice Parks

DEATHS

Miss Bernice Parks

Miss Bernice Parks died at her home at Justiceville Wednesday, December 11th, 1918, of pneumonia which developed from influenza, aged seventeen years. Funeral services were conducted at the Leemont M. P. Church, of which she was a member, by Rev. Howard Link on Friday, and interment was in Liberty Cemetery, Parksley, Va. She is survived by her parents, Mr. and Mrs. Thomas Parks, and two brothers, Messrs. Grover and Charles Parks

Peninsula Enterprise 21 December 1918 – She is incorrectly identified as Bernice, who had died in 1911.

Herbert Burton Parsons

Herbert Burton Parsons.

Herbert Burton Parsons, eight year old son of Mr. and Mrs. W. C. Parsons, of Onley, Va., died at the home of his parents on Sunday, December 15th, of pneumonia. Funeral services, conducted by Rev. P. M. Hank, were held at the home on Tuesday, and interment was in Edge Hill Cemetery, Accomac. He is survived by his parents, one brother, William, his grandparents, Mr. and Mrs. William A. Burton, of Onley, and Mrs. John D. Parsons, of Atlantic. He was a bright and attractive child and his death was a great shock to his family, who have the sympathy of many friends in their bereavement.

Peninsula Enterprise 21 December 1918

Edith Mae Beatty

MRS. MAE BOWERS BEATTY.

Mrs. Mae Bowers Beatty, wife of Roland M. Beatty and daughter of Mr and Mrs. H. C. Bowers, of 927 Twenty-seventh street, died at noon on Tuesday at her home at Cape Charles, Va., of pneumonia. Deceased was born in this city on October 3, 1881. She was married sixteen years ago to Mr. Beatty and since then she had resided at Cape Charles, Va., where her husband is employed as chief clerk in the Pennsylvania Railroad company offices at that place. She was a member of the Presbyterian church. Besides her husband she is survived by three children: Elizabeth, Kenneth and Catherine. She is also survived by her husband, one brother, Frank, and a sister, Mrs. Irene, wife of E. E. Buller, of this city. The remains will be brought to this city today and taken to the home of her parents from which the funeral will be held at 4 o'clock Friday afternoon. Interment in Rose Hill cemetery.

Lula V. Jester

Miss Lullie Jester died December 17th of pneumonia, aged twenty years. She was a fine young lady and was very talented. Her death was a shock to the whole community. She is survived by her parents, Mr. and Mrs. William Jester, Jr., one brother and two sisters.

The schooner W. H. Meekins with

Peninsula Enterprise 19 January 1919

Claud J. Matthews

Mr. Claude J. Matthews, son of Mayor and Mrs. A. F. Matthews, died December 19th, of pneumonia, aged 33 years. He was a promising young man, and well thought of by all who knew him. He was a graduate of our High School and later took a business course at Poughkeepsie, N. Y., On finishing his course at the latter school he was elected cashier of The Farmers and Merchants Bank of New Church. In this position he was efficient and popular. Some months ago he enlisted in the Naval Reserve, and had not been discharged at the time of his death. Mr. Matthews was prominent in Masonic circles, being a member of Temperanceville Lodge. Besides his parents, he is survived by one sister, Mrs. O. T. Baynard, and one brother, Mr. Charles F. Matthews.

Peninsula Enterprise 4 January 1919

Mary C. Andrews

Mrs. Mary Andrews died on the 18th of December of pneumonia, aged forty-four years. She is survived by her husband, Mr. George Andrews, one daughter and mother and father.

Peninsula Enterprise 4 January 1919

Joseph Kellam

Mr. Joe Kellam.

Mr. Joe Kellam died of pneumonia at the home of his father, Mr. S. T. Kellam, near Painter, Va., on December 25th, aged 50 years. He was a member of Pungoteague Methodist Church and was well thought of by all who knew him. Funeral services were held at Pungoteague Methodist Church on December 27th, conducted by his pastor, Rev. Mr. Odell, and burial was in the family burying ground. His father, Mr. S. T. Kellam, and one brother, Mr. William Kellam, survive him.

Peninsula Enterprise 4 January 1919

Annie Eliza Davis

Mrs. Major T. Davis.

Mrs. Annie Davis, widow of the late Major T. Davis, died at the home of her daughter, Mrs. Quincey E. Justice, Tuesday, January 7th, of pneumonia, aged about sixty-eight years. Funeral services were conducted Thursday afternoon by Rev. Mr. Walker, pastor of New Church Baptist Church, of which she was a member, and interment was in the Nelson Cemetery, near New Church, Va. Mrs. Davis is survived by one daughter, Mrs. Quincey E. Justice, and one son, Mr. Mornay Davis, of Wattsville.

Peninsula Enterprise 11 January 1919

Mary Ann Martin

Mrs. Mary Hyslop Martin

The community of Cradockville was greatly shocked Monday morning when the sad news went around that Mrs. Mary Hyslop Martin had died that morning between eight and nine o'clock, after a short illness of pneumonia as a result of the "flu". Her condition was not considered serious until Sunday and she began to grow worse rapidly Sunday afternoon, and all that nurses and doctors could do could not save her. Her work on earth was done and Our Heavenly Father called her to be with Him. She was twenty seven years old and the only child of Mr. and Mrs. W. H. Hyslop, who with the husband have the sympathy of the entire community. Besides her husband and parents she leaves two little girls, Frances aged five years and Virginia aged two years. Funeral services were held at Craddockville church, of which she had been a member since she was a child, Tuesday afternoon at 2 o'clock, conducted by her pastor, Rev. W. A. Wright, and she was laid to rest in the Belle Haven cemetery. The floral tributes and the size of the crowd were evidences of the esteem in which she was held. The active pall bearers were Messrs C. B. Kelly, Ray Wise, A. M. Kellam, Charlie Mason, Marvin Custis and Forrest Davis, Honorary, Messrs Roy Kellam, W. N. Copes, Finney Hyslop, Will Mason, Charlie Davis, Elmer Roland and Mal Kellam.

Peninsula Enterprise 25 January 1919

Olevia May Steelman

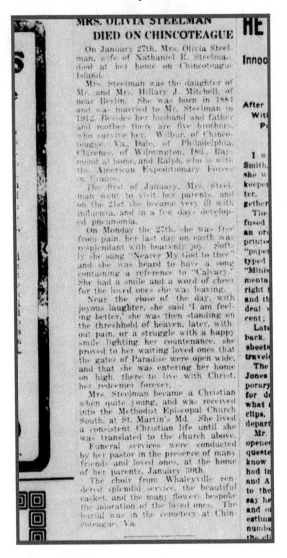

MRS. OLIVIA STEELMAN DIED ON CHINCOTEAGUE

On January 27th, Mrs. Olivia Steelman, wife of Nathaniel R. Steelman, died at her home on Chincoteague Island.

Mrs. Steelman was the daughter of Mr. and Mrs. Hillary J. Mitchell, of near Berlin. She was born in 1881 and was married to Mr. Steelman in 1912. Besides her husband and father and mother there are five brothers, who survive her, Wilbur, of Chincoteague, Va., Dale, of Philadelphia, Clarence, of Wilmington, Del., Raymond at home, and Ralph, who is with the American Expeditionary Forces in France.

The first of January, Mrs. Steelman went to visit her parents, and on the 21st she became very ill with influenza, and in a few days developed pneumonia.

On Monday the 27th, she was free from pain, her last day on earth was resplendant with heavenly joy. Softly she sang "Nearer My God to thee" and she was heard to have a song containing a reference to "Calvary." She had a smile and a word of cheer for the loved ones she was leaving.

Near the close of the day, with joyous laughter, she said 'I am feeling better,' she was then standing on the threshhold of heaven, later, without pain, or a struggle with a happy smile lighting her countenance, she proved to her waiting loved ones that the gates of Paradise were open wide, and that she was entering her home on high, there to live with Christ, her redeemer forever.

Mrs. Steelman became a Christian when quite young, and was received into the Methodist Episcopal Church South, at St. Martin's, Md. She lived a consistent Christian life until she was translated to the church above.

Funeral services were conducted by her pastor in the presence of many friends and loved ones, at the home of her parents, January 30th.

The choir from Whaleyville rendered splendid service, the beautiful casket, and the many flowers bespoke the adoration of the loved ones. The burial was in the cemetery at Chincoteague, Va.

Democratic Messenger, Snow Hill, MD - 15 February 1919

Charlotte Alice Gladding

Miss Alice Gladding.

Miss Alice Gladding died of pneumonia at her home at Horntown, Va., on Friday, January 24th., aged sixty years. She was a member of Horntown Baptist Church for a number of years. Funeral services were held on Sunday conducted by her pastor, Rev. A. C. Walker, and interment was in the family burying ground at Miona. She is survived by one sister, Mrs. Melvin Bloxom, and two brothers, Messrs James and John Gladding.

Peninsula Enterprise 1 February 1919

Margaret and Ione Scott

Mrs. Iona Fitchett Stott.

Mrs. Ione Fitchett Scott, wife of Mr. W. C. Scott, died at her home near Seaview Wednesday morning, after a brief illness of Influenza, aged about 28 years. Burial services were held at the grave in Cape Charles Cemetary, Friday afternoon.

Her little 2 year old child, who was sick with the influenza, lived only a few hours after the death of its mother.

Mrs. Scott is survived by her husband mother Mrs. W. C. Fitchett and brother, Mr. Granville Fitchett, of Cheap Side.

Peninsula Enterprise 1 February 1919

Fannie Thomas Bell

Mrs. Fannie Thomas Bell.

Mrs. Fannie Thomas Bell, wife of Mr. Bayly A. Bell, died at her home near Birds Nest, Wednesday afternoon of pneumonia, aged about 36 years. Funeral services were held at Red Bank Baptist Church, Friday afternoon, conducted by Rev. W. W. Reynolds. Interment in the church cemetery.

She is survived by her husband and two children, Bayly, Jr., and Margaret her father Mr. Ben Thomas, brother Mr. Harry Thomas and sister, Miss Nola Thomas.

Peninsula Enterprise 1 February 1919

Thomas C. Carpenter

Mr. Thomas Carpenter died Monday of pneumonia, which developed from influenza, aged forty-eight years. He is survived by his wife and two children.

Peninsula Enterprise 15 February 1919

Ansley Hopkins

Mr. Ansel Hopkins died last Thursday of influenza aged thirty-six years. He is survived by his wife.

Peninsula Enterprise 1 March 1919

References

Barker, Stephanie Forrest - The impact of the 1918-1919 influenza epidemic on Virginia (Master's Thesis) – University of Richmond - 2002

Carpenter, James Waine Sr. – **Chincoteague Island – A History of Local Businesses** – Loco Dare Press – 2014

Carpenter, James Waine Sr. – **From Tears to Memories, The Cemeteries of Chincoteague** – Loco Dare Press – 2017

Dickon, Chris – **Eastern Shore Railroad** – Arcadia Publishing – 2006

Klugman, Keith P., Astley, Christina Mills, Lipsitch, Marc - **Time from Illness Onset to Death, 1918 Influenza and Pneumococcal Pneumonia** - Emerg Infect Dis. 2009 Feb; 15(2): 346–347

Mariner, Kirk – Off 13, The Eastern Shore of Virginia Guidebook – Miona Publications - 2016

Treese, Loretta – **Railroads of the Eastern Shore** – Arcadia Publishing – 2021

Starko, Karen M. - **Salicylates and Pandemic Influenza Mortality, 1918–1919 Pharmacology, Pathology, and Historic Evidence** - Clinical Infectious Diseases, Volume 49, Issue 9, 15 November 2009, Pages 1405–1410, https://doi.org/10.1086/606060

Virginia Department of Health - **All Virginia, U.S., Death Records, 1912-2014** – Ancestry.com

Epilogue

How bad was the Spanish Flu pandemic compared to the current Corona virus pandemic? Looking only at the United States, 675,000 people died of the Spanish Flu out of a population of approximately 103,208,000 which is 0.65%. That took place in a period of about seven months.

As of today in October 2021, the United States has lost 773,834 people from the Corona virus out of a total population of 333,156,663 which is .23% and that took about 18 months.

The Spanish Flu killed at least 211 residents of the Eastern Shore of Virginia. Covid-19 has taken the lives of 119 residents, as of October 24, 2021.

Our ability to treat the effects of the Corona virus and the introduction of effective vaccines greatly reduced the death rate compared to what it might have been. However, we are still in the midst of the Corona Virus Pandemic, so the final toll is unknown.

CPSIA information can be obtained
at www.ICGtesting.com
Printed in the USA
LVHW051605110222
710784LV00014B/2428